CW00643819

Life is confusing enough, and that' head around the person and work <del></del> what we need is some clarity: Wh about God the Spirit and how do <del></del> <del></del> <del></del> today? To answer such questions *Breath of Life* offers just the help we need. A perfect introduction to the subject it is both readable and practical. The book walks us through the bigger picture of the Bible, showing us how the coming of the Spirit is the fulfilment of God's plan, and then helps us see what God's word says on all it means for us to keep in step with the Spirit as he works in our lives and in the life of the church. Expect to learn, expect to grow, expect to discover all it means for you to rejoice in the greatness of the Spirit.

Neil Powell
Pastor,
City Church, Edgbaston, Birmingham.

With so much confusing noise around about the Spirit and the 'spiritual', Orlando Saer's book is an answer to a Christian's prayer. He cuts through the cacophony with Biblical wisdom and gives us reason for confidence – and joy! – in the person and work of the one called 'the breath of God'. It is a book that made me smile – not just because it is written with good humour but because it reminded me of the way God makes me new.

Michael Jensen
Rector,
St Mark's Anglican Church,
Darling Point, New South Wales.

Although it is more than fifty years since the charismatic movement first burst into evangelicalism, there still remains much confusion and misunderstanding amongst Christians about the Holy Spirit, true spirituality and the normal Christian life. Orlando Saer's short book cuts through this confusion and enables us to hear what the Bible has to say about the person and the work of the Holy Spirit. Writing in a punchy and engaging style, he sets the work of the Spirit in the context of God's unfolding plan of redemption, and shows how he fulfils his new covenant promises to bring us new life, new speech, new power and a new heart. He does not duck the difficult questions, for example about tongues and miracles, but addresses them head-on in a balanced way through clear biblical exegeses, and provides helpful illustrations and practical applications. Anyone who reads this book will be moved to rejoice afresh in the work of the Holy Spirit, to love Jesus more, and to develop a true spirituality in which they use their gifts to serve his church and extend his mission to the world.

JOHN STEVENS
National Director,
Fellowship of Independent Evangelical Churches,
Market Harborough, Leicestershire

BREATH
OF
LIFE

**Rediscovering the Holy Spirit
and Following His Lead**

ORLANDO SAER

CHRISTIAN
FOCUS

Copyright © Orlando Saer 2017

ISBN Nos:
paperback 978-1-78191-980-4
epub 978-1-52710-011-4
mobi 978-1-52710-012-1

Published in 2017
by
Christian Focus Publications Ltd.,
Geanies House, Fearn, Ross-shire,
IV20 1TW, Scotland, Great Britain.

Cover design by Paul Lewis

Printed by
Bell and Bain, Glasgow

CONTENTS

To five remarkable young men I'm privileged to call my godchildren: Barnaby Frith, Joshua Gibbs, David Kellahan, Tom Rees and Zach Whitehouse. May each of you learn what it is to keep in step with the Spirit throughout your lives. Follow his lead!

INTRODUCTION

OK so admit it. You've had the same thought. At least if you've ever experienced air travel.

You've got off the plane after a bumpy flight. You're bleary-eyed. Groggy. You've trudged along miles of airport corridors on your way to the baggage hall. There's not a trolley in sight, so you're left to stagger along under the weight of your various bags, as you try and work out how to cover the last few miles of your journey.

That's when the self-reproach begins.

'Why can't I learn to pack light like everyone else?'

'How could I have forgotten which bus to take?'

'Why didn't I ask someone to come and pick me up?'

And then you see them. The meet-and-greet crew. The limo services. With their placards – 'Jones', 'Edith Higton + party', 'Dr Kazinski'. And their unspoken promises of a comfortable ride home.

And you begin to wonder.

What if…

This guy has never met Dr Kazinski. He hasn't a clue what Dr Kazinski looks like. What if you were to go up to him and claim a ride? The temptation is sweet. Your guard is down and your inner risk-taker causes you to entertain the thought for a little longer than you should…

'Let me take that for you, Dr Kazinski.'

And in a moment, he's got the lot. The suitcase, the wheely bag, the duty-free. He leads the way. You follow behind, empty-handed, even smiling – all the more as you spot those envious looks on the faces of less fortunate passengers around you.

The chauffeur opens the door for you to his cavernous limo. And you start to make yourself comfortable – stretching out on the back seat, enjoying the drinks cabinet.

Eventually you pull up outside the Ritz Hotel. The concierge whisks you in, takes your bags and spirits you up to the Queen Victoria Suite on the top floor, where you throw yourself on the four-poster bed and start checking out the room-service menu…

Meanwhile, the real Dr Kazinski is left cursing under his breath. The no-show from the limo service leaves him with no choice. He heads outside and piles on to the smelly number 17 bus with the riff-raff. Half an hour later, with creased clothes and punctured pride, he's dropped outside some dodgy hostel in Hounslow.

OK, wake up. Time to get back to reality. Where's that bus?

Ah, come on – I know you've thought about it!

Ponder that situation for a moment. What happened – in your little daydream at least – was a fairly simple phenomenon.

A red-carpet welcome was shown to the wrong person. Which led to the 'right' person being left out in the cold.

Why did it happen? You were dishonest, yes. But more than that, the driver was naïve and gullible.

He should have had a picture on his phone of the real Dr Kazinski – and checked your face against that picture. Or at least he should have had a signature, a passport number, a password. Something.

He should have ID'd you more carefully than he did.

The world being what it is, it was inexcusable just to take your word for it. He should have made sure the red-carpet welcome he was offering – the bag-carrying, the limo-ride, the suite at the Ritz – was being offered to the right guy.

This book is all about the Holy Spirit – and it's written with a sneaking suspicion in the back of my mind.

Churches routinely welcome the Spirit into their midst. And individual Christian believers earnestly welcome the Spirit into their hearts and their lives. In a manner of speaking, the red carpet is laid out. 'Come right in! Step inside our limo here! Make yourself at home!'

But here's the suspicion. It's that things may not be quite what they seem. The one purporting to be the Spirit – or even introduced to us by well-meaning Christian friends as the Spirit – may not live up to the name. And, the world still being what it is, it's *we* who are naïve and gullible if we always take things at face value.

Where I hope you'll get to by the time you've finished this short book is to have some kind of 'picture on your phone' of what the real Spirit looks like. Some kind of ID detail. A basic idea of what you should expect to see if you're dealing with the genuine article. So that when some experience comes along with the 'Spirit' label attached to it, you've got something reliable to check the claim against.

That way, you'll avoid welcoming in the wrong guy. And you'll make sure you really do lay out the red carpet to those things that are truly of the Spirit.

THE SPIRIT'S CREDENTIALS

What kind of things am I talking about here? What are these things Christian people identify with the Spirit but which might in fact turn out to have dubious 'Spirit' credentials? There are many, but let's start with three.

1. Spontaneous and informal

Kate is an enthusiastic young Christian. She's moved to a new town. And she's checking out churches in the search for a new spiritual home. She decides to tweet her experiences week by week so her friends can follow her progress.

> Kate Philip
> @ChurchSearch
> Oxdale Community Church today. Nice.
> Really Spirit-led. No preacher – everyone
> just spoke as prompted. Worship just
> went with the flow.

It's a well-worn equation. Spontaneous equals 'Led by the Spirit'.

Church A has the whole running order of its services pre-planned. Maybe even pre-printed for the congregation. The preacher has worked out the talk or sermon ahead of time. Maybe it's even scripted. The songs have been chosen ahead of time – and practised.

Church B has only a loose sense of programme. The speaker looks to be prompted on the spur of the moment.

Other people join in if they've got something to say. Someone just starts singing – and the band take their lead from that.

Which of these two is 'led by the Spirit'? The answer's obvious, isn't it?

Or maybe not.

You personally might appreciate an atmosphere of spontaneity and informality in a church. It might tick all the right boxes for your particular temperament and preferences. A whole church might even share those preferences and decide to give a red-carpet welcome to these values. But is that really what the Bible means by 'led by the Spirit'?

Not even close.

You want to know what that expression *does* mean? Keep reading!

> Kate Philip
> @ChurchSearch
> Oxdale Christian Fellowship today.
> Another winner. Exuberant. Dancing. Even
> the preacher was in tears. Whole place
> filled with the Spirit.

2. Emotional and expressive

There's something striking about a bunch of people who aren't afraid to show their emotions. They're obviously 'keeping it real'.

And equally, there's maybe something a bit disappointing about a crowd of seeming emotional corpses. You know the type. Hands folded. Eyes dry. Upper lips stiff.

But here's the question: is the first group *really* 'filled with the Spirit'? Maybe they are. But if so, that heart-on-your-sleeve emotional exuberance has little to do with it. You can find emotional exuberance at a football game. The truth is: people of different personalities and cultures show what's going on in their hearts in different ways – some more obvious than others. But whether people express their emotions openly or not is a very different question to whether they're Spirit-filled or not – that's something totally different, as we'll see later.

Just because you see 'emotionally expressive', don't conclude 'Spirit-filled'.

> Kate Philip
> @ChurchSearch
> St John's Oxdale today. Amazing. Serious about gifts of Spirit. Healings. Tongues. Someone had a word of knowledge for me – by name!

3. Weird and dramatic

Most of us are wowed by apparently inexplicable things. Someone arrives at church with one leg longer than the other, and goes home dramatically healed? It gets our attention. Someone who's a normal, rational accountant in the week suddenly starts speaking gibberish on a Sunday morning. We're intrigued. Someone we've never met gives us a how-could-she-possibly-have-known-that-about-me kind of message. We're stunned.

Weird stuff. Dramatic stuff. It makes us sit up.

But should these things make us think: 'gifts of the Spirit'? Possibly. But not necessarily. When you get what the Bible has to say about gifts of the Spirit, you might find yourself looking in slightly different places.

Just because you see 'weird' or 'freaky', don't think 'spiritual gifts'!

Kate Philip
@ChurchSearch

Logos Church Oxdale today. Well-organised operation. Had a charismatic split thirty-five years ago, so they don't mention the Spirit at all, just in case. Really wise.

4. Divisive and unnecessary

It's quite understandable. The memory of a painful episode in the church's history lives on. It was a time when relationships were strained to breaking point. In fact a group upped and left to start another church down the road. And it was all to do with the Spirit.

Decades have gone by, but for some it still feels raw. Why bring up the Spirit now? Church seems to go on fine without recourse to that kind of language. Why take a risk? The Spirit is surely best left unmentioned.

But can that be right? When you work out what the Spirit is really about, you're likely to start celebrating his work and thinking more about unity than about division.

Just because 'Spirit' talk is avoided on the grounds of 'divisiveness', don't think 'wise' or 'sensible'!

In the course of this book, we'll think about all those 'Spirit' expressions – and many more. But we're going to try and get beyond what the average Christian means by them – to what the *Bible* means by them. Why? Because if the Bible really is the work of the Spirit, and it's the Spirit we want to learn about, we've got a pretty obvious place to turn. We'll hear it from the horse's mouth!

1

THE BACKSTORY

If you really want to understand the Spirit of God, the place to start is obvious. You start with the very verses where those 'Spirit' expressions come from. Right? That's a no-brainer, isn't it?

What are some of those phrases?

- 'Led by the Spirit'. OK, let's turn to Romans 8.

- 'Filled with the Spirit'. Ephesians 5 here we come.

- 'Sealed in the Spirit'. We'll have to look up Ephesians 1.

- 'Walking by the Spirit'. Now we're off to Galatians 5.

- 'Praying in the Spirit'. Scroll down to Ephesians 6.

And on it goes. These are the places where the expressions are introduced. So they're the best places to start, right?

Wrong.

Suppose I asked you about your wife (or your girlfriend or husband, boyfriend, mother, or just someone who means a lot to you: change the illustration to fit!).

I said to you: tell me about her, and what she means to you.

And you came back with something like this: 'Well, she's 5 foot 4. She's got brown hair. She's always cold. And when she thinks nobody's looking, she likes dancing to One Direction.'

I'm sorry, but you haven't really answered my question. A few facts and statistics aren't going to help me all that much in understanding a person. I need more. It's too superficial a way of telling me about a person. I need you to go deeper.

Or suppose I asked a university professor, 'What is history?'

And she came back to me: 'Well, in 1066 William the Conqueror won the Battle of Hastings. In fourteen hundred and ninety-two, Columbus sailed the ocean blue. And in 1957 I was born.'

I'm going to be left disappointed. All she's told me are some things that happened in history. Big things, I grant you. (Well, two of them, anyway.) But they don't really give me an idea of what history itself is.

I guess we're going to have to go further back than the verses where those 'Spirit' slogans appear. We'll get to them, obviously. But we're not in a position to understand a verse which mentions the Spirit if we don't yet know who or what the Spirit is!

16

So maybe we need to go back to the big day itself. Go to that climactic moment of the story of the Spirit when – for the first time ever – the Spirit was poured out widely and dramatically, with thousands of people turning to Christ as a result. Go to Pentecost.

I would think that counts as a big day. And – as I say – even the climax of the story.

But here's the thing about climaxes. You can't appreciate a climax if it comes right at the beginning. In fact, if it's right at the beginning, it's hard to think how it could even *be* a climax.

So let's get this straight. If you want to understand the Spirit of God, it won't even work to start with Pentecost. If you're going to get into a story, the place to start is not at the dramatic climax, but at the beginning.

And so it's to the beginning we will go. And when I say the beginning, I *mean* the beginning!

It starts with the first eleven chapters of the Bible. That's where we find the problem to which the rest of the Bible provides the solution. It's when the first representatives of humanity decide to shut God out of their lives – and when, to their horror, they find that his response is to shut them out of his.

But here's where we get to the interesting bit. It's the *language* that's used for what happens.

Speech

First thing that actually happens in the entire Bible? It's that God *speaks*. 'Let there be light', he says (Genesis 1:3).

It's also the first thing that human beings do in the Bible. Adam's first recorded action was to look at God's creation and to give names to what he sees: 'whatever the man called each living thing, that was its name'

(Genesis 2:19). He even names his companion: from Genesis 2:23 on, the fairer sex is called 'woman'.

So far, so good. But it's all about to change. Before long, it's their words which will lead both of them astray. First the snake speaking to Eve:

> Did God really say...? (Genesis 3:1)

Then Eve speaking to Adam: God's judgement will now come down

> ...because you listened to your wife (Genesis 3:17).

Disaster. That great God-imitating thing that human beings do – speaking – has mutated into a God-*defying* thing.

And there's worse to come.

By Genesis 11, this gift of speech has hardened into a totally rebellious, even treasonous thing. The people of the day use it to plot a coup.

> Then they said, 'Come, let us build ourselves a city, with a tower that reaches to the heavens, so that we may make a name for ourselves' (verse 4).

At which point even the patience of God runs out. And he acts in judgement. But here's the thing. *It is specifically a judgement on their speaking and communication.*

> Come, let us go down and confuse their language so they will not understand each other (verse 7).

Hence the name of the city: 'Babel'. It's where our word 'babble' comes from. From that day on, when people spoke to each other it sounded like mere babbling.

So if God is going to restore humanity and reverse the effects of the fall, it's becoming clear what will be needed.

From Genesis 12 on, as we read the Bible, we're going to be on the lookout for any sign of *a new ability to speak –* some kind of human speech that is *for* God (not against him), *about* God (not about ourselves), and *enabled by* God (since it was he who effectively disabled it).

Is it going to happen? Will God provide this new speech?

I know where you want me to go at this point. You want me to fast forward to Pentecost. You're itching to get to the good bit.

Slow down. There's a big chunk of plot to cover before we get there! Remember, you can't appreciate – or indeed understand – the climax until you've seen what goes before.

Apart from anything else, there's a second issue that needs resolving.

Heart

There's an issue that runs even deeper than speaking. It's the human heart.

Rewind for a moment to that fateful scene in the Garden of Eden. We need to take a closer look. We need to spot what exactly it was which led Eve to eat that forbidden fruit.

> When the woman saw that the fruit of the tree was good for food and pleasing to the eye, and also desirable for gaining wisdom, she took some and ate it. She also gave some to her husband, who was with her, and he ate it (Genesis 3:6).

There are two forces at war here. There is God's earlier instruction *not to* eat it. But now there is also her inclination *to* eat it. Which wins out – the instruction or the inclination? It's the latter. What she *wanted* trumps what God *commanded*.

Sound familiar in your life?

It's bad, but not as bad as it's going to get.

As the years go on, the attitude becomes hardened. By the time of Noah it's practically concrete:

> The Lord saw how great the wickedness of the human race had become on the earth, and that every inclination of the thoughts of the human heart was only evil all the time (Genesis 6:5).

Notice how the human heart is no longer dithering. There's no more weighing up good and bad. Now it's *constant* ('every inclination'). It's *consistent* ('all the time'). It's thoroughly *corrupted* ('only evil'). And the verdict is *comprehensive* ('the human race').

Let's be clear on what we're talking about here. We tend to use the word 'heart' to describe our emotional life. To talk about head versus heart is to pit our rational side versus our touchy-feely side. But that's not what 'heart' means in the Bible. Someone's heart – in Bible terms – is the centre of their being. It's the core of who they really are and what they're really about.

So the heart of every individual – the very centre of each person who walked the planet – has by this point become utterly turned against God.

If the rest of the Bible is going to show us God fixing the problem, what is needed? It's not tough to see. It's nothing short of *a new heart*.

But we're not done yet with this catalogue of horror. You might think that – as the old saying goes – the heart of the problem is the problem of the heart. But it gets worse!

Life

I'm not an especially creative person. The odd carpentry project is about as far as I go in that department. I'm in awe of artists and composers and sculptors who can bring new works into existence. But even they are no match for God. God is full of creativity.

What's interesting is that he goes about his work in different ways. In Genesis 1, it's all speaking:

'And God said, "let there be X", and there was X.'

'And God said, "let there be Y", and there was Y.'

But when it comes to Adam, things get shaken up a bit. Instead of speaking him into existence, God opts for a different procedure: breathing.

> Then the Lord God formed a man from the dust of the ground and breathed into his nostrils the breath of life, and the man became a living being (Genesis 2:7).

Let me put it like this. The life that was breathed into that first human being was the life of God himself. From the very beginning, we were made to share in the divine life.

The point is made even more clearly by the landscaping of the garden. Right in the middle of it stood a tree. There were lots of other trees, but this one was special. It was the 'tree of life'. A symbol of the eternal life, the divine life, for which we were made.

But along with that tree stood another. One with a 'Do not disturb' sign hung on it.

> You are free to eat from any tree in the garden; but you must not eat from the tree of the knowledge of good and evil, for when you eat from it you will certainly die (Genesis 2:16-17).

Sure enough, they do eat from the tree. And, sure enough, they start dying. Genesis 4 sees the first death – as Cain kills Abel. But then, suddenly, it's everywhere. It becomes the repeated refrain of Genesis 5.

Then he died… then he died… then he died…

But it's not just physical death. Real life in the Bible is not a matter of brain stem activity. It's a matter of relationship with God himself. So the worst kind of life to lose would be life with God.

That's what happens in Genesis chapter 3. Adam and Eve are banished from the garden. No more of that walking with God in the cool of the day. That's history now. Dead and gone.

And just to make sure nobody misses the point, God takes some fairly high-octane security measures. He puts his beefiest bouncers in place 'to guard the way to the tree of life' (verse 24). The 'access all areas' pass is hereby revoked.

Life is over. Death is normal. Spiritual death is an unavoidable reality. That's the human predicament as we leave those early chapters of Genesis.

What's needed is clear. Humanity is crying out for *a new way of living* – living with God. The question is left hanging there: where will this new life come from?

If you're anything like me, you're just itching to flick forward to Pentecost and the end of the story. But don't do it. Not yet. There's one more problem we need to see, if we're going to get the full picture.

Power

Power is fairly easy to define. It's the ability to make things happen. The more you can make happen, and the less effort required to do it, the more power you have. So to have absolute power is to be able to make anything happen by doing nothing more than speaking.

That's God in Genesis 1. He speaks, and the cosmos comes into being.

But God doesn't keep all the power to himself. He invests human beings with a measure of power. That's what the whole naming operation is all about. Adam says it's to be called this or that. And that's how it is. Adam has God-like power over creation.

It's not going to last forever, though. Among the other effects of the human rebellion, the power of humanity over creation is reduced. Seriously reduced.

> Cursed is the ground because of you; through painful toil you will eat food from it all the days of your life. It will produce thorns and thistles for you, and you will eat the plants of the field. By the sweat of your brow you will eat your food (Genesis 3:17-19).

It's not hard to see what's happened here. If power is the ability to make things happen, and the more you can make happen with less effort, the more power you have, then take a look at this. Human beings now make less happen, and it takes more effort to do it.

Humanity's power over the earth is on the down.

And God isn't finished yet.

Think back to the end of these miserable chapters. The building of Babel. It wasn't just about speaking. It was also about power. That's the real problem God sees with what's going on there. And it's what he wants to have stopped.

> But the Lord came down to see the city and the tower the people were building. The Lord said, 'If as one people speaking the same language they have begun to

do this, then nothing they plan will be impossible for them' (Genesis 11:5-6).

That's the key word: impossible. 'Nothing… impossible for them'. Scattering them around the world was God's way of dealing with that. Divide and conquer. Kill collaboration. Take the power away.

So the full horror of the human situation is becoming clear. This is a fourth great need we're going to be looking to see addressed as we read on in the Bible. Not just new speech, a new heart and new life. But *a new power* too.

How on earth is God going to fix all this? Can it in fact be fixed at all?

Now, I know what you're thinking: 'Can we get on to the Spirit now? Please? I don't mind a bit of the backstory, but seriously – we're still in the book of Genesis?'

Hang in there. If you've ever found yourself absolutely parched, you will know how wonderful the taste of water can be.

I once trekked what's been claimed to be the deepest canyon in the world – Southern Peru's Colca Canyon. The claim is questionable, but it's still a decent hike down and then up again. Here's where I went wrong: I went solo, and I took no water. Yes, yes, I know. Stupid.

It wasn't so bad going down. But on the way back up, without the generosity of fellow-hikers offering me the odd dribble, I don't think I would have made it. Two things kept me going: the extraordinary sight of the condors gliding above me (with a wingspan of 10 feet, they are truly magnificent, and they did their best to distract me from the thirst), and the prospect of water at the village at the top. Never in my life has water tasted so good as when I got back!

Let me urge you: allow yourself to feel the thirst of Genesis 1-11 – and feel it well – before running for the water of Acts 2.

In fact, there are still some twists and turns along the path to be negotiated before we get there.

A FRESH START

In Genesis 12 God makes a fresh start with humanity. He issues a series of promises – a 'covenant' – with Abraham (or Abram as he was known then). And he repeats it and reframes those promises a couple of times in the chapters that follow.

That new start begins to take shape in the book of Exodus, as God gathers together his people around Moses.

But what's interesting is the *shape* of that fresh start, and what he does with Moses. And *how* he does it. What does Israel get in Moses?

Fresh speech

For a start, they get a leader who is given *a special power of speech*. He's uniquely equipped to speak for God!

When you go for a job interview, the normal dynamic has you wanting to convince the interviewer to give you the job. Right? Well it seems Moses didn't get the memo on that one.

At the burning bush God reveals his name and promptly commissions Moses to lead Israel out of Egypt. But here's the thing. Moses doesn't want the job! Why not? Because he doesn't have the gift of the gab. He just doesn't have a way with words.

> Moses said to the Lord, 'Pardon your servant, Lord. I have never been eloquent, neither in the past nor since

you have spoken to your servant. I am slow of speech and tongue' (Exodus 4:10).

But God is having none of it.

> The LORD said to him, 'Who gave human beings their mouths? Who makes them deaf or mute? Who gives them sight or makes them blind? Is it not I, the LORD? Now go; I will help you speak and will teach you what to say' (verses 11-12).

This is especially striking when you come to think of where things got to in Genesis 11. God is doing the very thing we saw was needed. In Moses, he is making possible a new kind of speaking – a way of speaking *for* God and *enabled by* God.

Moses isn't quite done with his efforts to turn down the job. He keeps trying his hand. So God graciously includes Aaron in the scheme. The two of them will have a job-share arrangement. A team ministry: Moses will do more of the listening, Aaron will do more of the talking. But the point is: between them, Moses and Aaron get the ability to speak for God.

It looks like the first instalment of this fresh start is well and truly in place.

New speech: tick. But there's more.

Fresh heart

There's also, with Moses, talk of *a heart for God*.

The story of Moses is in some ways the story of a massive anti-climax. He leads his people out of slavery in Egypt. He leads them safe and sound through the Red Sea. He leads them into victory in battle. He leads them into a covenant relationship with God at Mount Sinai. And then comes the great culmination – leading them into the Promised Land. Does he take them?

Er, no.

Why not? Because, when the people are on the verge of entering the land, there is rebellion in the ranks. As a result, the people are condemned to stay in the wilderness for forty years – until the whole generation has died – including Moses himself.

But before he goes, he gives a series of three speeches, which together make up the book of Deuteronomy. The speeches are really a kind of half-time pep talk. They're all focussed on one thing: preparing the people for how to live in the land. Their behaviour. Their words. Their attitudes.

One of the things they need is a good attitude to God.

> 'Love the LORD your God with all your heart, and with all your soul and with all your strength,' says Moses (Deuteronomy 6:5).

In other words, they need a whole new outlook towards God.

It's not the first time he's spoken in these kind of terms. He's said something quite similar before:

> If with all your heart and all your soul you seek God, you will find him (Deuteronomy 4:29).

Yes, I know. At this stage, it's only an instruction. It's not necessarily a reality. It's not as though we're told Moses – or anybody else for that matter – is actually seeking God with all their hearts. That said, it does seem to bode well. There is at least the *prospect* of God's people seeking and loving God with their hearts.

That great quest for a new heart for God's people seems to be homing in.

And it goes on.

Fresh life

Think of Moses and what comes to mind? If you know anything about him at all, you'll be aware that most of the key stories are full of another element – life out of death.

You see it in Moses himself.

Things looked bleak for him. He was born in the middle of a genocide. The instructions were clear: all Hebrew baby boys were to be drowned at birth. And yet, despite that, through an extraordinary sequence of events, Moses lives!

Life out of death.

You see it again in the ministry of Moses.

God used Moses to bring his people out of Egypt. But how? It was through that extraordinary event of the Passover. Pharaoh was a cruel and stubborn man. It took some effort to get his attention. In the end it took something quite terrifying: a death in every household. Every eldest boy in every home that night was struck dead.

But in the middle of it all, God had communicated via Moses a way by which the Hebrew people could dodge death.

> No destructive plague will touch you when I strike Egypt (Exodus 12:13).

Again, it was life in the midst of death.

And then there's the scene at the Red Sea. The people of Israel are trapped. Pharaoh's army behind them. The Sea in front of them. Not a great set of options on their menu. 'Which would you prefer, Sir: death by sword or death by drowning?'

But God has other plans. He sends another waiter to serve them, name of Moses. Through Moses, God provides a way through death to life.

The Israelites went through the sea on dry ground, with a wall of water on their right and on their left. That day the LORD saved Israel from the hands of the Egyptians, and Israel saw the Egyptians lying dead on the shore (Exodus 14:30).

Yet again, with Moses around it's life out of death.

You can't really miss the fact that this is a fresh start. There are ticks against not just the new speech we've been looking for, but also the new heart and the new life.

And then there's the power. Extraordinary power.

Fresh Power

There was power in the signs that Moses did to sell himself to his people. If he was going to be accepted as their God-given leader, he had to prove his credentials. That's what we see in Exodus 4.

> ➤ *Look at this: my staff has turned into a snake!*

> ➤ *Look at this: it's back to a staff again!*

> ➤ *Look at this: my hand has turned leprous! Now it's back to normal! Now the river water has turned into blood!*

I think I'd be convinced. There's only one credible explanation: Moses was able to perform all these powerful signs *because God was working in him.*

Then there are the plagues (Exodus 7-12). The blood and the frogs and the gnats and the flies – and the rest. Terrible blights. But they're more signs of God's power at work in the ministry of Moses.

And as time goes on, there are no signs of the power drying up. Far from it, there's a whole series of fresh expressions of God's power. Could you part the Red Sea as Moses did (chapter 14)? Could you lay on a daily feast of manna, or produce water by striking a rock, or defeat an army by raising your hands (chapters 15–17)? Didn't think so.

In Moses, there is unimaginable power at work – God's power.

The source

One thing's for sure. Something big is going on here. This fresh start is no damp squib. It's really happening. But how?

The answer should be obvious. It's because of God's Spirit.

The point is not laboured. It just seems to be taken for granted. But there's a moment of clarity hidden away in the Book of Numbers.

Just before the first attempt to enter the Promised Land, there's a get-real moment about Moses and his leadership. He needs to get more serious about delegation. He needs to involve others in the work he's been doing. The time has come to share out the leadership.

What's involved in that? Not a cabinet meeting. Not a training weekend. Instead, it's the passing on of God's Spirit.

> God 'took some of the power of the Spirit that was on Moses and put it on the seventy elders' (Numbers 11:17).

And so it all becomes clear. *This is how Moses was able to be so dramatically used in God's fresh start with his people. All along, the power of the Spirit of God was on him.*

That speaking he and Aaron could do, that new heart he could promote, that new life he brought, that power he demonstrated – it was all the work of the Spirit.

Meet God's change agent. The one who brings God's fresh starts. The one who's always there when things are made right.

He's called the Holy Spirit.

And it's because of him – as we'll see during the rest of this book – that God's people experience each aspect of that fresh start. We'll take them in a slightly different order. But we'll look at each in turn. New life. New speech. New power. New heart.

2

THE SPIRIT GOES GLOBAL

THE entertainment world is littered with one-hit wonders.

Think of Paul Hogan. The first Crocodile Dundee movie was an enormous hit, and at the centre of it was the iconic role of 'Mick'. Hogan's looks, charm and funny accent created a perfect storm of popular acclaim. The Golden Globe he bagged made a sequel inevitable, even though it was somewhat less warmly received. In fact the franchise even limped to a third film (which went straight to video).

The role certainly set him up for life: he ended up marrying his co-star. But movie-wise, he's done virtually nothing of note since – unless you count a role in 'Flipper' and a series of commercials for the Australian Tourist Commission, inviting Americans to come 'down under'.

He's almost the archetypal 'one-hit wonder'.

So here's my question: was the Holy Spirit a one-hit wonder? Clearly Moses was a great hit for the Spirit. But did the story end with him?

By the time this chapter ends, we should be in a good position to answer that.

But before we get to that, maybe we need to take a step back. Because there's a question hanging there: who or what actually *is* the Spirit?

WHAT DOES 'SPIRIT' MEAN?

There's not been much mention of the Spirit so far in our journey through the Bible. Or has there? Actually, there has, but you could be forgiven for missing it.

The Spirit makes an early appearance on to the scene. Right at the very start of Genesis – even before creation begins – the Spirit is there: 'Darkness was over the surface of the deep, and the Spirit of God was hovering over the waters' (Genesis 1:2).

It's not much to go on. But it's a helpful reminder about what 'spirit' actually means.

Are you ready for some jargon? In the Bible, 'Spirit' is the translation of two words. In the Old Testament, which was mostly written in Hebrew, it's the word *Ruach*. In the New Testament, originally in Greek, it's the word *Pneuma*. *Pneuma* probably rings more bells with you, because it's sitting there at the heart of some English words we know – pneumonia, pneumatic drills. Things like that.

Both words mean exactly the same thing: 'wind', 'breath', or 'air'. That's why God's Spirit is moving over the waters in Genesis 2 – his Spirit is like the wind moving over the waves.

In fact, *Ruach* often appears in your Bible as just that: 'breath' or 'air'.

34

- When God walks in the garden in the cool of the day, it's actually the *Ruach* of the day, the 'airy' time of day (Genesis 3:8).

- When the animals trot up into Noah's ark, it's pairs of all creatures that had the breath of life in them: the *Ruach* of life (Genesis 7:22).

- When God wants the flood to subside, he causes a wind to blow over the earth: a *Ruach* (Genesis 8:1).

And so on.

So *Ruach* just means breath, wind or air.

As the Bible goes on, though, many more details are added to the picture. For example, it turns out that the Spirit is a person, not just a force.

It's very easy to lapse into talking about the Spirit as an 'it' rather than a 'he'. Something like a 'force', maybe. Or a 'power'.

Actually that's not entirely wrong: the Bible does seem to talk of the Spirit in impersonal ways sometimes: even in the New Testament, the Spirit is described as like fire, water, oil, wind and even a bird.

But not always. The Spirit also behaves like a person. He's involved in speaking, in teaching, in testifying, and in leading people. He searches and he knows. He can be grieved and blasphemed. The Spirit is most certainly more a 'he' than an 'it'. He's a person.

And he's a divine person at that. In time he would be repeatedly associated with the other two members of the Godhead: the trio includes the Father, the Son and the Holy Spirit (e.g. Matthew 28:19). Lying to the Holy Spirit is the same as lying to God (Acts 5:3-4). For the Holy Spirit to speak is for God to speak (Hebrews 3:7; 4:7).

But how can a 'breath' or a 'wind' be a person like this – let alone God himself?

As we read on, we find that *Ruach* also comes to mean somebody's 'spirit', that is the inner essence of a person. Or even the inner essence of God himself.

We finished the last chapter with a glimpse of Moses, the great bringer of God's fresh start. And we asked the question: how was he able to do his work? The answer is that – as well as his own spirit – he also had God's Spirit on him. He was the first great man of the Spirit!

But was he the last? Or to put it another way, was the Holy Spirit a one-hit wonder?

The answer is, of course, no. There were others.

THE SPIRIT ON SHOW

Take Joseph. He of the stylish clothing. Joseph was a great example of that first effect of the Spirit: *Spirit-given speech for God*.

As he languished in prison, he probably didn't see a summons to Pharaoh coming. But one day that's exactly what he got. He's invited – that's a nice way of putting it – to interpret the dreams which have been troubling Pharaoh.

No problem. This is his line of work. It's a piece of cake for him. He explains what God is going to do, the exact time frame, and the winning strategy to adopt in the light of what's coming. In a way, he's a forerunner of all the Old Testament prophets that would make their appearances later on – Elijah, Elisha, Isaiah and Jeremiah, and all that crowd.

And Pharaoh's just gobsmacked. Check out his response when he hears Joseph talking like this:

> Can we find anyone like this man, one in whom is the Spirit of God? (Genesis 41:38).

Notice how even a spiritual outsider can discern evidence of God's Spirit at work simply from hearing Joseph *speak*.

Or look at King David. Now there's a character with feet of clay. He went from hero to hedonist almost overnight. But the humility that marked him out in the beginning did return. Eventually. And as it did, he showed to the watching world (that's you and me) that second effect of the Spirit: *a Spirit-given heart for God*.

The offence was a serious one. He has sex with a married woman. Then gets her husband killed so as to be able to make things permanent with the girl. In time, though, he is brought to his senses. And Psalm 51 is his prayer of confession. He asks for cleansing. And then he goes on:

> Create in me a pure heart, O God, and renew a steadfast spirit within me. Do not cast me from your presence or take your Holy Spirit from me (verses 10-11).

Did you spot the connection? A pure heart, a heart focussed on God, is a mark of God's Spirit being with him.

And what about Job, the great sufferer? Yes, you guessed it. He's going to show us an example of that third effect: *Spirit-given life.*

Actually if there's one thing Job was likely an expert on, it's not life but death. He lived to see his entire household slaughtered. He was certainly no stranger to grief.

Maybe that's why his words about life – and where it comes from – are so striking:

> The Spirit of God has made me, the breath of the Almighty gives me life (Job 33:4).

Here is Job, looking in the mirror. And what does he see as he looks at his life? Evidence of the Spirit at work.

Bringing up the rear in our little quad of Old Testament characters who knew what they were talking about when it came to the workings of God's Spirit is Samson. His particular area of expertise was that fourth effect: *Spirit-given power.*

Take a look at this guy. He is just ice-cool. He spots the girl of his dreams and heads out for a first date with her. It's hard to know what kind of preparations he's made in terms of his appearance, but whatever trouble he went to, one thing's for sure: it didn't show. Because on the way to meet her, he bumps into a lion.

That lion is in the wrong place at the wrong time.

> The Spirit of the Lord came powerfully upon him so that he tore the lion apart with his bare hands as he might have torn a young goat (Judges 14:6).

And then – without even stopping to straighten his tie or brush that long hair of his – it's on to the date. He's as cool as a cucumber: 'Then he went down and talked to the woman, and he liked her.'

You've got to have respect for this guy. It's as though nothing's happened! But of course it has. It takes superhuman strength to kill a lion with your bare hands. But we're told explicitly where the power came from: it was God's Spirit who provided it.

And it's the same thing all over again in the next chapter. Samson is tied up with ropes. This is likely some pretty serious strapping down. They know the kind of person they're dealing with in Samson, so they're not going to take any chances. But what happens?

> The Spirit of the Lord came powerfully upon him (Judges 15:14).

He bursts out of his restraints – and promptly goes and kills a thousand men.

Bottom line? Moses wasn't alone in experiencing first-hand the workings of God's Spirit. There were others who were affected.

But there's one thing you can't miss about these various experiences. Yes, they all experience the Spirit. But they're the exception, not the norm. In other words there are just *certain people* who experience the Spirit. And the experience is only to equip them for *certain roles*. And more often than not, it's only for *certain periods of time*.

Surely there's got to be a fuller experience of the Spirit than this?

OPEN ACCESS TO THE SPIRIT?

Technology moves fast. It wasn't so very long ago that if you wanted to find someone who (a) had a computer, (b) had an internet connection and (c) knew how to use his or her computer to access the internet, you'd have had to look hard. Maybe very hard. Yes, such people existed, but they were few and far between. And they could only connect in specific circumstances, like when they were hardwired into a phone line. And even if they could go online, there were only a limited number of functions they would be helped with.

Now we've entered a whole new era. Anyone can pull their phone out of their pocket and they're online in seconds.

That's the kind of step-change we're waiting for here.

There's clearly some way to go along the road before we reach our Acts 2 destination – and the talk there of mass access to God's Spirit. But we're getting closer.

As the history of Israel gradually unwinds, things go south. There's civil war, and idolatry, and greed and hypocrisy, and… the list goes on. And eventually things reach crisis point. God uses first the Assyrians and then the Babylonians to turf his people away from their homes. It looks like curtains for the people of Israel and Judah.

But despite what they might think, God hasn't given up on them. In fact, God is committed to starting all over again with this people. It will be a radical rebooting of the relationship. So radical, in fact, that it's called a 'New Covenant'. It's going to involve a whole new way of relating to his people.

He tells his people all about it in a whole string of prophecies. And if you read those prophecies carefully, one thing hits you between the eyes.

Drum roll, please.

Central to this reboot, this 'new covenant', is the way in which God's people will experience God's Spirit.

Coming soon: new speech for all

First of all, the Spirit would work in God's people – and *all* of God's people – a new speech. In the reboot, the privilege of speaking for God wouldn't be restricted to just a select few (Moses and a handful of other spiritual celebrities). No. Everyone would speak for God.

Listen to the prophet Joel quoting God:

> I will pour out my Spirit on all people. Your sons and your daughters will prophesy, your old men will dream dreams, your young men will see visions. Even on my servants, both men and women, I will pour out my Spirit in those days (Joel 2:28-29).

40

It's quite a prospect that Joel holds out here. Somehow, sometime, every member of God's people will not only be given divine understanding and experience, but also be able to *share* that understanding and experience with others. In fact, the words will just well up inside them and tumble out. The Spirit will make it possible.

Coming soon: a new heart for all

But there's more. In the reboot of God's covenant relationship with his people, the Spirit's arrival would achieve something else. It would make possible for all of them a whole new heart, one focussed on God.

The prophet Ezekiel quotes God on this:

> I will sprinkle clean water on you, and you will be clean; I will cleanse you from all your impurities and from all your idols. I will give you a new heart and put a new spirit in you; I will remove from you your heart of stone and give you a heart of flesh. And I will put my Spirit in you and move you to follow my decrees and be careful to keep my laws (Ezekiel 36:25-27).

Close your eyes for a moment and switch on your imagination. Imagine you're one of the first people to hear this prophecy. There you are, an exile in Babylon. You've been manhandled, turfed out of your house and marched away from Jerusalem by some babbling hooligan. Now you're in unfamiliar surroundings and far from home. And you're still stunned – just totally *stunned* – that God really would follow through on his threats and punish his people like that. It's still sinking in that the whole reason you're here is because you and your ancestors simply failed to live for God. You and they failed to keep your side of the covenant.

Why, oh why didn't we listen?! We had our good days, but we just couldn't seem to stay faithful. And now we're here. This is our terminus – me, my family, my nation. Even if God were to give us another chance, we'd muck it up. Because obeying God just seems so hard to keep up!

But now you hear this. God is going to start again. He's going to reboot his relationship with you. Only this time it won't be just on the basis of some impossible-to-keep bunch of rules and regulations. No, this time he's going to do the microwave thing: work from the inside out. His Spirit will reach inside and change your very heart. He'll make you *want* to obey! Won't that be something!

Coming soon: new life for all

In fact it's going to mean a third effect – new life for all God's people.

In the very next chapter of Ezekiel (chapter 37), something very weird takes place. At least, it's not something you'd see every day around my neck of the woods.

The prophet Ezekiel is taken to a valley which has one odd feature to it. The ground is covered – with bones! Ezekiel is no stranger to bizarre instructions. But he must have raised an eyebrow at this one. He's told to start talking to these dead bones.

And when he does, the strangest thing happens. It's almost like a horror movie. The bones start moving. Soon it becomes clear they're moving towards each other. Full skeletons are being reassembled. Then flesh starts growing on these skeletons. And then they come to life.

I did warn you!

But what God later explains is that the whole extraordinary experience is really just an elaborate visual aid. It's a picture of what he's going to do with his people in the future. He's going to give them new life – and that will be just as dramatic as what Ezekiel has just experienced.

> This is what the Sovereign LORD says: 'O my people, I am going to open your graves and bring you up from them; I will bring you back to the land of Israel. Then you, my people, will know that I am the LORD, when I open your graves and bring you up from them. I will put my Spirit in you and you will live, and I will settle you in your own land' (Ezekiel 37:12-14).

The Spirit, in other words, will bring new life to God's people. Soon.

Coming, er, when?

The question is: *how* soon is all this coming?

Presumably it would be when the exile was over. That would be the most obvious timing.

A few decades after these prophecies, in a series of 'waves', some of the exiled people did start to go home to Jerusalem. They resettled the city and began to rebuild it.

But when they did, there were disappointments all round. The people behaved barely any better than they had before. The city and the walls looked less impressive than before. And there isn't really this experience of the Spirit that might have been expected. In fact, everything's a bit flat.

One thing's for sure. This can't be it! *We have surely not yet reached the dawn of the wonderful new age when the speech-supplying, heart-transforming, life-giving Spirit would be poured out on all God's people!*

43

Have you ever played hide-and-seek in the woods with a young child? If you have, you might have noticed that they're usually better at judging direction than distance. Go and hide a couple of trees away from them, and call out to make their seeking easier. And then carefully peer behind and watch the show. You'll see them rush forward in the right direction, but only get as far as the first tree. They look around the tree, preparing for a moment of triumphant discovery. But their face turns to confusion as they find nobody there. It's only then that they reassess and look on to the second tree and spot you!

They're better at direction than distance. And so are we.

We've been looking in the right direction. But we thought our quest would be over when we got to the first tree, the end of the exile. We thought that's when we'd see the wonderful fulfilment of all those prophecies about the new dawn and the Spirit that would be poured out.

We were wrong.

And now we're getting very close indeed to the climax of the story – the Day of Pentecost.

But there's one final stop on the way we still need to make. So far, we're three down and one to go. We've seen that the 'reboot' will involve new speech, a new heart and a new life. What was that fourth effect of the Spirit?

Coming soon: new power for all

It's in Acts chapter 1 – the chapter before Pentecost.

There's something strange about the beginning of Acts. So many of the great prophecies of the Old Testament have been fulfilled in the life and the death of Jesus. But even now, after the resurrection, there's a sense of waiting. In fact, the risen Jesus appears to his friends and makes that waiting mandatory.

Do not leave Jerusalem, but wait… (Acts 1:4).

Wait for what?

Wait for the gift my Father promised, which you have heard me speak about.

What's that then? Which gift is he talking about?

In a few days, you will be baptised with the Holy Spirit.

So that's it. They're waiting for the Spirit. And what will happen then?

You will receive power when the Holy Spirit comes, and you will be my witnesses…

That's good to hear. We've been waiting since Genesis 11 to see the lost power widely restored to human beings. And it's about to happen. Any moment now, the wait will be over.

PENTECOST

At last, it's time to look at Pentecost. We're finally in a position to appreciate and understand what really went on on that much-celebrated day. It's been a long time coming, but we really needed the backstory if we're going to get it.

So, Pentecost. What happened?

The myths about Pentecost

First, some things that *didn't* happen at Pentecost.

Myth #1: 'The first Christians initiated Pentecost'
Wrong. Pentecost was a regular Jewish festival. One of the Big 3. It was also known as the 'Feast of Weeks' (it

happened 7 *weeks* after Passover). And it was first and foremost their harvest festival.

Just as the farewell meal of Jesus took place on a Jewish festival day (Passover), so the arrival of the Spirit did.

Myth #2: 'There was fire and wind at Pentecost'
Not so. There was a lot of noise, and it must have had that kind of 'rushing' sound to it. Because when Luke casts around for something to compare it to, he says, 'There was a sound like the blowing of violent wind'. Note that word 'like'. No actual wind. Just a wind-like noise. Same with the fire. What they saw was what 'seemed to be tongues of fire'. Key word: 'seemed'. In other words they weren't actually flames. The whatever-it-was just looked more like that than anything else.

Myth #3: 'They all began to speak a non-human kind of language'
Wrong again. Nobody started doing what people today sometimes refer to as 'speaking in tongues' (a non-rational language of the Spirit). No, they just spoke normal human languages. What was striking is that they weren't their own!

> All of them were filled with the Holy Spirit and began to speak in other tongues [i.e. languages] as the Spirit enabled them (verse 4).

Hence what happens for the crowd in verse 6:

> Each one heard their own language being spoken.

The reality about Pentecost

OK – there are some myths busted. Now then, what really did happen? In a nutshell, *everything we've been waiting for happened.*

As the Spirit is poured out, we see that *new speaking* we've been waiting for – the speaking for God, about God, enabled by God – and bypassing the communication problems put in place by God. Here's a new speaking which can be understood by others. Listen to the response of the crowd:

> We hear them declaring the wonders of God in our own tongues (verse 11).

All those language barriers that were put up at Babel are smashed down. There's no problem of confused languages any more. That new speaking has become a reality.

Just to make sure we don't miss it, Peter actually quotes Joel's prophecy:

> This is what was spoken by the prophet Joel… (verse 16).

What Joel said would happen is now happening – that's the message. This is it!

What else do we see when the Spirit is poured out? We see evidence of that *new heart* that we've been waiting for. By the end of the day, there's just the kind of response from the crowds every preacher dreams of:

> When the people heard this, they were cut to the heart (verse 37).

And they're ready to show it. They ask what to do in response, and Peter tells them straight:

> Repent [i.e. turn your hearts back to God] and be baptised.

And that's exactly what they do – in very large numbers: Three thousand people accept the message (verse 41). And before you know it, they're eating together *'with glad and sincere hearts'* (verse 46).

What else?

You know what's coming. As the Spirit is poured out, the *new life* we've been waiting for comes into view.

There's a twist here. As Peter explains the Pentecost event in his sermon, the new life he's interested in more than any other is the new life of the risen Jesus. The Spirit being poured out confirms that the resurrection really did happen.

How does that work? The logic's not hard to follow. It's because Jesus was risen (verse 32) that he could receive the Spirit from the Father (verse 33). And it's because he has received the Spirit from the Father that he can now pour the Spirit on us.

So centre-stage in all the drama of Pentecost is the new life of Jesus himself.

But Jesus doesn't hog all the new life for himself. Read on in the book of Acts and you'll soon see that new life overflowing to plenty of others. Repentance leads to new life.

Take Acts 11. Here's Peter describing an incident that happened when he took the gospel to some non-Jewish people.

> As I began to speak, the Holy Spirit came upon them (verse 15).

And the conclusion he draws from this response?

> So then, even to Gentiles God has granted repentance that leads to life.

The Gentiles? That's most of us! This new era sees new life on offer on a grand scale.

And the power? It's staring us in the face in the drama of Pentecost! As the Spirit is poured out, the power we've been waiting for is plain to see. The crowd's reaction says it all.

Bewilderment (verse 6).

Utterly amazed (verse 7).

Amazed and perplexed (verse 12).

And the power lingers. By the end of the chapter, acts of power are becoming routine.

Everyone was filled with awe at the many wonders and signs performed by the apostles (verse 43).

It's all there at Pentecost. All the questions asked by the first eleven chapters of Genesis have found an answer. That great and glorious, long-awaited reboot of God's relationship with his people has swung into action. The new era – the era of the Spirit – has come.

3

BRINGING JESUS TO US

CHRISTIAN people sometimes talk about having a 'relationship with Jesus'. But when others hear this language, they don't get it.

> 'What does that even *mean*, a "relationship with Jesus"? Where is he? How can you have a relationship with someone who died thousands of years ago?'

> 'Tell me: which of your five senses do you use to live out this relationship with Jesus? Can you see him? Hear him? Touch him? Smell? Taste? I have more of a relationship with my pillow than you have with Jesus, don't I?'

Where is this Jesus you have a 'relationship' with?

Maybe you've found yourself wondering the same thing on occasion. I certainly have.

But in truth, you could have asked that very question right back in the very first days of the Christian church in Jerusalem.

The Book of Acts helps us to get a handle on that time, but it's a strange name for a book, when you come to think about it. I mean, really: 'Acts'? It's like calling a book 'stuff that happened'.

Traditionally it's been known as 'The Acts of the Apostles', which is a bit more informative.

But consider two facts:

1. Acts is the second volume of a two-volume work (Luke-Acts). Even though our Bibles have John's gospel in between the two, they go together.

2. Acts begins with a summary statement: *'In my former book, Theophilus, I wrote about all that Jesus began to do and to teach until the day he was taken up to heaven'* (Acts 1:1-2).

You can't miss the implication. If the first volume was about what Jesus *began* to do and teach, the second volume must be about what he *continued* to do and teach. Maybe a better title for Acts would be 'The Acts of Jesus'!

But how does that make sense? Where is Jesus? There's a brief flashback to the ascension right at the start of the book. But just 9 verses into the very first chapter, Jesus is gone. *Really* gone. *Ascended-to-heaven-never-to-return-before-the-end-of-time* gone.

So how can Acts tell the story of his continuing presence?

Answer: as the book begins, the coming of the Spirit is predicted to happen any day now. We've already seen what the Spirit is going to do for people like us. But before that, the Spirit will have a vital role to play for Jesus himself. In a nutshell, one of the primary works of the Spirit is to *bring Jesus to the world.*

ENABLING THE MINISTRY OF JESUS

It was always going to be like this. Isaiah the prophet lived 800 years before Jesus, but he had lots to say about things that were still to come.

In chapter 11 he talked about a new kind of king who would emerge after the exile.

> A shoot will come up from the stump of Jesse… (Isaiah 11:1).

(That's just another way of saying this is going to be a descendant of King David: Jesse was David's father.)

> …from his roots a Branch will bear fruit.

As Isaiah goes on, he sets out the job description for this king. It's pretty impressive and wide-ranging.

> In that day the Root of Jesse will stand as a banner for the peoples; the nations will rally to him, and his resting place will be glorious (verse 10).

So this king will have an impact on his own people, the Jewish people. That's for sure. The reference to David makes that clear. But actually he's going to have an impact way beyond that. His influence will extend to the nations around too.

How can that be? How can one man exert such influence? We might well wonder. It all sounds a bit far-fetched. But the answer is given to us in black and white.

> 'The Spirit of the Lord will rest on him –
>   the Spirit of wisdom and of understanding,

53

the Spirit of counsel and of might,
the Spirit of the knowledge and fear of the LORD –
and he will delight in the fear of the LORD' (verses 2-3).

God's Spirit will rest on this new king. And it's by this Spirit that he will be able to go about his work.

So much for the coming king. But it's the same story with that other great figure Isaiah says is coming. In chapter 42 we meet the 'Servant' (sometimes known as the 'Suffering Servant' because of the familiar descriptions of his fate in Isaiah 53).

Here is my servant, whom I uphold, my chosen one in whom I delight (Isaiah 42:1).

We've already seen the role of the king. Now for the role of the servant.

'In faithfulness he will bring forth justice;
he will not falter or be discouraged
till he establishes justice on earth.
In his teaching the islands will put their hope'
(verses 3-4).

Again it's a huge job description. Justice for the whole earth! We're left aching to know how he will do it.

Isaiah doesn't leave us disappointed.

'I will put my Spirit on him,
and he will bring justice to the nations'
(verse 1).

So it's the same story again. It is God's Spirit who will make possible the international ministry of this servant, whoever he is.

We have to wait to see the King and the Servant. We wait until the end of the exile, but still there's not really any sign of them. Remember that game of hide-and-seek in the woods? We've gone in the right direction. But not for the right distance. It turns out the King and the Servant aren't behind that first tree. So we keep waiting until we get to a second tree. That is, the end of the 'spiritual exile'.

And there they are.

Only it's not quite how we expected things. It turns out, when you get to the New Testament, these two prophecies – about the majestic king and the suffering servant – are fulfilled in one and the same person! Both of them were describing ahead of time the person and work of Jesus of Nazareth.

Two prophecies. One combined fulfilment.

But one thing's for certain: this character *is going to be brought to the world by the Spirit.*

And guess what. That is *exactly* what we see when we open the gospels…

- How is Jesus even conceived in the first place?

Not in the usual way babies are made – that's for sure.

> The angel answered Mary, 'The Holy Spirit will come on you, and the power of the Most High will overshadow you' (Luke 1:35).

Right at the start, the man Jesus is brought to life by the Spirit.

- How is Jesus recognised for who he really is?

Despite the pictures you may have seen, it wasn't by the dinner plate levitating behind his head. Here is the meeting of the rather ancient Simeon and the eight-day-old Jesus:

55

...the Holy Spirit was on him. It had been revealed to him by the Holy Spirit that he would not die before he had seen the Lord's Messiah. Moved by the Spirit, he went into the temple courts... Simeon took [Jesus] in his arms and praised God, saying: '...my eyes have seen your salvation' (Luke 2:25-30).

You can't miss it. Jesus can only be identified by other people thanks to the Spirit.

- What will people experience when they get baptised by Jesus?

There's more to it than getting wet. John the Baptist baptises with water, but Jesus...

will baptise you with the Holy Spirit and with fire (Luke 3:16).

To be baptised by Jesus is to receive the Spirit.

- What will Jesus be given on the first day of his new job?

Something just a bit better than an ID card and a company email address.

...Jesus was baptised too. And as he was praying, heaven was opened and the Holy Spirit descended on him in bodily form like a dove (Luke 3:21-22).

At the outset of his ministry, Jesus receives the Spirit.

- How is it that Jesus receives guidance?

No sat-nav for him. Something way better.

Jesus, full of the Spirit, left the Jordan, and was led by the Spirit into the wilderness... (Luke 4:1).

Jesus was directed by the Spirit.

- How is Jesus resourced for his work?

You guessed it.

> Jesus returned to Galilee in the power of the Spirit (Luke 4:14).

Jesus was empowered by the Spirit.

- How does Jesus understand his ministry?

> The Spirit of the Lord is on me, because he has anointed me… (Luke 4:18).

Jesus saw himself as anointed by the Spirit.

And on it goes. You can't miss it. Jesus is brought to the world by the Spirit!

Or is he?

The world is a big place. What about the people who don't have the good fortune to live in Galilee and Jerusalem, and the rest of that tiny patch of the planet in which Jesus lived and moved about? What about people who live in some other place?

What about people who lived at some other *time* than that brief three-year period in which Jesus conducted his ministry? What about them?

More particularly, I guess we might want to ask, what about people like *us*? How could *we* ever get to benefit from Jesus? If the Spirit's about bringing Jesus to *us* (as in you and me specifically, in the here and now, rather than just 'someone'), how's he going to do it? How is he going to make sure we hear about him?

EXTENDING THE MINISTRY OF JESUS

The answer is that the same Spirit who was behind the ministry of Jesus in Judah and Galilee in the first century is sent to bring Jesus to the wider world. To extend his ministry, in other words.

Or to put it another way: some people got to experience the ministry of Jesus in person; the rest of us get to experience the ministry of Jesus by his Spirit. That's what the Spirit is really about. Bringing Jesus to us.

Jesus himself said as much in some of his last words to his followers.

> When the Advocate comes, whom I will send to you from the Father – the Spirit of Truth who goes out from the Father – he will testify about me (John 15:26).

The Spirit's role, in other words, will be to give the apostles the helping hand they need by telling them all about Jesus. And yes, they'll certainly need all the help they can get on this front. Why? Because their job is going to be to witness to Jesus. They've got to preach, teach, persuade, defend… and indeed write.

It's a big job. The whole story of Jesus needs to be told. In fact, more than that. The whole of what we call the New Testament has to be written! They've got a good start. They have their own eyes and ears. Their memories. But they'll need help beyond that, because it's got to be absolutely right. Absolutely true.

And that's where the Spirit comes in.

> … when he, the Spirit of truth, comes, he will guide you into all the truth (John 16:13).

This is big for us. Apart from anything else, if 'all truth' wasn't something the apostles had at that point, it means we're actually better off experiencing Jesus now, in the age of the Spirit, than people who heard Jesus first-hand. That puts a new perspective on things!

Jesus goes on to explain the process.

> He will not speak on his own; he will speak only what
> he hears, and he will tell you what is yet to come. He will
> glorify me because it is from me that he will receive what
> he will make known to you. All that belongs to the Father
> is mine. That is why I said the Spirit will receive from me
> what he will make known to you (John 16:13-15).

So in brief, the role of the Holy Spirit is to bring glory to
Jesus as he transfers the truth from Jesus to the apostles.
He'll make sure the apostles know all that needs to be
known about Jesus, so that they in turn can pass it on to
people like us.

In other words, the work of the Spirit is to make sure
the apostles have all they need so that everything about
Jesus can be brought to a bigger audience.

My Mum is a publisher. She's been in PR or publish-
ing her whole adult life. You may think that's a fairly un-
objectionable career. But just you try having a publisher
as a mother. Every time I've ever passed an exam, it's
in the paper. Every time I've gone abroad, or come back
from abroad, or got a prize or an award or done anything
that might merit a passing comment, it's in the paper. If
a passing Martian landed on earth, and for some reason
wanted to put together a biography of me, he could probably get everything he needs from surveying the archives
of the *West Sussex Gazette*.

OK, I'm exaggerating a bit. But that's what publishers
and PR people are about – they're about getting the
biggest audience for the subjects they have an interest in.

And that is what the Spirit does for Jesus and his
teachings. He extends them to people who live in times
and places other than his own.

THE SPIRIT WILL GUIDE YOU INTO ALL TRUTH?

When Christians read the Bible, we often expect it to apply very directly to us. So some people have read verses like John 16:13 ('The Spirit… will guide you into all truth') as a direct promise to Christians today of direct and reliable communication from God. The implication is that if we can clear our minds and discern the Spirit speaking to us directly, we will come into God's perfect truth.

There are a number of reasons why this is not great Bible-reading. The most obvious is that, when Jesus spells out the mechanism the Spirit will use for guiding 'you' into all truth, it turns out to involve the use of *memory*.

> …the Advocate, the Holy Spirit, whom the Father will send in my name, will teach you all things and will <u>remind</u> you of everything I have said to you (John 14:25).

Guess what? You can't be reminded of something you never knew! The point is: the Spirit will teach and guide *the apostles* (and *only* the apostles) about Jesus through helping *them* to recall perfectly what they've already witnessed.

That doesn't mean there's no application to us. There is. But the application is not to look to be led into all truth directly (bypassing the apostles); but to trust what the apostles and their circle say when we read the New Testament. Because when they wrote, they were guided by the Spirit into all truth.

THE SPIRIT AND THE BIBLE

If you're interested in the whole publication procedure for God's truth, it's spelt out more fully in 1 Corinthians 2.

Here you find the apostle Paul putting the pieces together.

Paul is unimpressed with the people society regards as 'experts'. They actually don't have a clue about God. If you look to philosophers and scientists and politicians and boffins to find out about God, you'll be sorely disappointed.

Why? Because the most important truth in the universe is *a mystery that has been hidden* (1 Corinthians 2:7).

So the world's experts have never been able to work it out.

> None of the rulers of this age understood it, for if they had, they would not have crucified the Lord of glory (verse 8).

But there is good news.

> What no eye has seen, what no ear has heard, and what no human mind has conceived – the things God has prepared for those love him – these are the things God has revealed to us... (verses 9-10).

In other words, don't fret. You and I don't need to remain in the dark about this 'mystery' forever. God has taken the initiative to tell us about himself, his purposes, his plans and so on.

It's actually one of God's major character traits. He loves to speak!

Revelation – as it's called – is just what God does. And the way he does it is via his Spirit.

> These are the things God has revealed to us by his Spirit (verse 10).

We get to see how it works in the verses that follow. There are four stages:

1. The Spirit reads the mind of God.

> The Spirit searches all things, even the deep things of God. For who knows a person's thoughts except their own spirit within them? In the same way, no one knows the thoughts of God except the Spirit of God (verses 10-11).

In other words, the Spirit has the whole scoop on God and his thoughts. We'll come to how that is later on. But that's the first stage of the revelation process. The Spirit reads the mind of God.

2. The Spirit communicates this to the apostles.

> What we have received is not the spirit of the world, but the Spirit who is from God, so that we may understand what God has freely given us (verse 12).

So the Spirit has acted to make sure the apostles understand the mind of God.

3. The apostles communicate it to everyone else.

> This is what we speak, not in words taught us by human wisdom, but in words taught by the Spirit, explaining spiritual realities with Spirit-taught words (verse 13).

The apostles have a job to do. It's to get communicating. It doesn't matter whether they do it in person (like Peter's speeches in Acts) or in writing (like the New Testament we have in front of us). Either way, when they communicate to people like us, they're saying what the Spirit has taught them.

And then finally…

4. The hearers are enabled by the Spirit to accept what they hear from the apostles.

> The person without the Spirit does not accept the things that come from the Spirit of God, but considers them foolishness, and cannot understand them because they are discerned only through the Spirit (verse 14).

If you haven't got the Spirit in you, then you'll never really get it. That's presumably why there are some very brainy people around who just can't seem to grasp even the most basic teachings of the Bible.

And there are, aren't there? You might know someone like that. You tear your hair out because you don't see what the problem is.

Why can't they just get it?

The problem is they need more than brains to get it. They need the Spirit.

Do you see how the Spirit works from both ends, as it were, to make sure good communication happens? He's there at the 'transmitter' end. And he's at the receiver end too! He works from *God's* end, enabling the apostles to say the right things. And he works from *our* end, making sure we recognise the truth of what they say.

What's in view here is what we call the New Testament. But make no mistake. The Spirit was just as involved in the earlier parts of the Bible too.

In 2 Peter 1, the apostle Peter is calling for attention to be paid to both the New Testament and the Old. Why the old? Simple. It's because…

> Prophecy never had its origin in the human will, but prophets, though human, spoke from God as they were…

Ready for it?

…as they were carried along by the Holy Spirit (verse 21).

That word 'carried along' is a technical term. It's from the world of sailing. It's what happens when the wind fills the sails of a boat and moves it along its course as a result.

That's what happened with the Old Testament writers. The Spirit carried them along: he stood behind them and filled their sails as they set about their writing. Just as he stood behind the New Testament writings of the apostles.

THE MIND OF CHRIST

Where does all this leave us? We've looked at three passages (John 16, 1 Corinthians 2, 2 Peter 1) which set out the Spirit's work of opening up Christ to us and indeed the thoughts and plans of God himself. The result of this work is summarised at the very end of 1 Corinthians 2.

It comes down to six amazing words. Are you ready for them?

…we have the mind of Christ! (verse 16).

Just allow those words to soak in for a minute.

The great work of the Spirit is a work on behalf of Jesus. It's to enable and extend the ministry of Jesus. To bring Jesus to us, so that we can think his very thoughts!

The Spirit got the ministry of Jesus off the starting blocks – right from his conception through to his preaching and people's reactions to him. That got things as far as the earthly ministry of Jesus.

But then the Spirit went further and put the ministry of Jesus out there in the public domain. He brought Jesus to people who lived in another time or place by enabling the apostles to put the ministry of Jesus (and the wider thoughts of God too) into words.

And that has left the apostles, and now *us* who read their writings, effectively being able to say 'We have the mind of Christ'!

The Spirit's work then: to bring Jesus to us. He is the great revealer!

THE SPIRIT TOLD ME...

We've seen how the Spirit works to show us Jesus – and the thoughts of God – in the Bible. But what about direct revelations? Should we expect the Spirit to communicate things to us apart from the Bible?

In some Christian subcultures, there is much talk of Spirit-given 'words of knowledge', or 'words from God', or 'prophecies' or 'visions'. By which is meant some communication from God other than the Bible.

What should we make of this? Can God communicate in such ways?

Here are six brief thoughts

1. Of course he can!

We have it on record that God has spoken through a donkey, through writing on a wall, through dreams and visions, and all sorts. When Philip met the Ethiopian on the Gaza Road, it was a result of a direct communication of the Spirit: 'The Spirit told Philip, "Go to that chariot..."' (Acts 8:29).

God can speak any way he chooses. But...

2. He doesn't need to.

By the later books of the New Testament, there's pre-cious little talk of direct communications of God by his Spirit. Why is that? Apparently because God's written word should be enough. In 2 Timothy 3:16 we're told how useful Scripture is – for teaching, rebuking, cor-recting and training in righteousness. And then Paul goes on (verse 17): 'so that the man of God may be thoroughly equipped for every good work'.

Scripture is all you need to live life God's way. What's more…

3. He hasn't promised to.

There are heaps of promises and assurances in the Bible. We've seen some of them already, like about how the Spirit will guide the apostles into all truth. But there's not a single one where God says he will direct normal believers in any other way than his written word.

We're given no expectation of it. And therefore…

4. It's down to God if he wants to.

There's no reason for us to look for some direct communication from God. There are some Chris-tians who spend their lives worrying that they might miss out on some particular word from God. My advice to them is: relax!

If God wants to tell you something in some unusual way, you can count on him to make sure you don't miss it!

5. Be discerning!

Obviously if God does clearly communicate some-thing to you, then take heed. Don't disregard anything

God has to say! But be open to the possibility that actually it's not his voice at all you are hearing.

Test it – is it in line with the Bible? Is it in line with wisdom?

Let me give you a couple of examples of how that kind of testing is needed.

I met a minister a few years ago. He was telling me his story. And it turned out he had heard the Spirit telling him directly to go into ministry. But his wife wasn't able to stand with him. 'I just can't make this step with you. If you go into ministry, that will be the end of our marriage', she said repeatedly. He knew she meant it, but he felt such a strong sense of the Spirit's leading that he pressed ahead anyway. The marriage ended as he knew it would, but he felt at peace because he'd pursued 'God's call on his life'.

Was it really the Spirit telling him to go into the ministry? Not a chance! You strip away the religious talk ('my calling'), and it just comes down to his deciding to ditch his marriage in favour of his preferred career. If he'd tested it, he'd have found the Bible says marriage is a lifelong commitment.

He was misled.

That's an example of testing it by the Bible. What about testing by wisdom?

A couple of old friends of mine – Tim and Abbie – were praying together one day. They were just friends, but shared a deep interest in the work of the Spirit, so used to talk and pray a lot. On this occasion they were praying together about their future marriages. But afterwards Tim confessed to

Abbie: 'as I said that word "marriages", I realised that the "marriage" bit was of the Spirit, but the "–s" bit was of the flesh. If we'd been praying fully in the Spirit we would have prayed for our future marriage – singular. Which means we must be meant to marry each other.'

And so they did!

Well, that's certainly one way to propose. But God has given us minds and he has instructed us to pursue wisdom in our decision-making, not to bypass the process of thinking.

Zapping us with a remote control from on high is just not God's style.

6. Be sensitive

Different Christian subcultures have different habits of speaking to describe the same thing. A thought comes into Bill's head and he'll immediately say, 'The Spirit told me'. A thought comes into Becky's head, and she'll say, 'I had an idea'. They may both be describing the same experience. But they jump different ways when it comes to understanding and expressing its significance.

If you push Bill, you find he's quite open to the possibility that it's not actually the Spirit, even though that was his first impression. If you push Becky, you find she's open to the possibility of her idea being prompted by the Spirit, even though she's bit more tentative.

That's all well and good. A lot of the differences between Christian subcultures come down to language. But because there are these differences, we need to be sensitive to the way in which we express ourselves to fellow believers.

Think about it. To say 'The Spirit told me' to someone unused to speaking in those terms could come across as plain manipulative. I mean, where can you go from there? To argue back is to argue with God!

'God told me to share a house with you next year'.

'God told me that you're going to give me a job'.

'Er, well, he hasn't told me that!'

Here's the key thing.

It's not unspiritual to talk in non-Spirit terms.

The apostle Paul sometimes talked about the Spirit speaking to him, or preventing him from something. But other times it's just 'it seemed good'. Or he 'didn't think it wise'. There's no fixed way of describing thought-processes in Christian decision-making. What is fixed is that we love each other. And that means we'll be careful to avoid alienating, misleading or manipulating other believers by the way we speak.

That said, if after careful consideration, comparing what's been said with the Bible, listening to godly wisdom from brothers and sisters, and so on, you do think what someone says is from God, then please – whatever you do – act on it! Take it to heart! Respond in an appropriate way!

RESPONDING

What we've seen in this chapter is that the major work of the Spirit is to bring Jesus to us. More specifically, he brings the teaching of Jesus and indeed all that God wants to reveal to us, so that we end up with the mind of Christ!

So how do we respond to all this? Let me suggest just two ways that being truly Spiritual will show itself.

1. To be Spiritual is to make much of Jesus.

Hang on a moment. To make much of *Jesus*? Is that a typo? Surely the man or woman of the Spirit will first and foremost make much of the *Spirit*. That's what you meant to say, right?

Wrong. I get that it seems counter-intuitive for a book all about the Spirit to be saying you really ought to be thinking less about the Spirit and more about someone else. But that's what the Spirit wants.

The truly Spiritual person will take his or her lead from the Spirit. If the Spirit wants to show you the Son, it's only respectful to him to let him do it!

Imagine you're at the theatre one night. You come in, take your seat and wait for it to start. The house lights go down. You hear some footsteps on stage. But then… nothing. There's total silence and utter darkness.

What's going on? You know the actor's there on stage. But it strikes you for the first time that if you're going to benefit from tonight's performance, you're going to need someone else to be in place.

You need the tech guy.

You need someone to do the lights. Make sure the spotlight is always on the actor's face. And you need someone to handle the sound, to get the PA system operating so you can hear the actor's voice. Happily, just at that moment, the show begins. On goes the spot and up goes the volume. And you know for sure the tech guy's here. Because the actor's face is lit up. And his voice is amped up.

What do you do now? You wouldn't think to look up at the tech box, would you? Partly because you know the guy's there – because you see the effects of his doing his job. But partly too because he (or his predecessors) set up your seat to face the stage, to face the actor. He doesn't want to be looked at.

He just wants to light up the actor's face, and amp up the actor's voice.

Because he knows that's the way for you and everyone else to see and hear the one on stage.

If you can get that picture, you've got what the Spirit is about. Not 'look at Me, listen to Me'; but 'look at him; listen to him'. He's bringing Jesus to us.

So sit back and enjoy the spectacle!

That's going to mean a number of things. Like…

• Taking time to think about the attractiveness of the character of Jesus.

  Is that something you spend much time on? Do you allow the Spirit to walk this extraordinary man off the page into your mind? How about specifically…

• Reflecting on his selfless service of others, or his big-heartedness towards the marginalised?

  The New Testament doesn't just list the fruit of the Spirit, it shows it to us in the person of Jesus. Love, joy, peace, patience. It's all there in 3D. Have you let your inner eye be bowled over by the Imax 3D presentation?

• Homing in on what he accomplished in terms of changing history?

The great journey from heaven to earth, to humanity, to the cross, to the tomb, to glory – all of it to bring his people back to their God? Do you meditate deeply and often on this, and allow meditation to lead to awe and praise and worship?

Delight in Jesus. Make much of him. Look where the Spirit is pointing and revel in what you see. Share in the ambition of Paul expressed in Philippians 3:10: 'I want to know Christ…'

2. To be Spiritual is to dig deep into God's word.

As we saw above, it's possible to respond to the work of the Spirit in superficially appropriate ways – but then realise that you're missing the whole point of the Spirit!

How about this as an example: you could respond to the Spirit communicating with you by communicating back to him. That makes sense, right? Complete the conversation. Make it a two-way street. Close the loop.

Is speaking to the Spirit in prayer the right response to the Spirit speaking to you in the Bible?

Well, it's tricky. The Spirit is a person, no doubt about that. The Spirit can hear – we've seen that. More than that, the Spirit is God – and God is certainly who we pray to.

And yet… there's not a single example in the whole of the Bible of someone praying to the Spirit. Not one. A couple of times people pray to the risen Jesus. Like in Acts 7:59 – where Stephen commits his spirit to his Saviour before he dies. But praying to the Spirit? Never.

If the Spirit is behind the whole Bible and he doesn't see fit to give us a single case of somebody speaking to him, well that sounds like a bit of a hint to me.

The Spirit certainly has a role in prayer – as we'll see in a later chapter. But that role is to help us speak to the Father.

If you want to be truly Spiritual in your response to the Spirit communicating with you, here's how. Don't speak back. Listen harder!

Or to put it Paul's way: 'Take… the sword of the Spirit, which is the word of God' (Ephesians 6:17).

The sword of the Spirit is part of the equipment given to us to help us in our daily fight to put Jesus first. And it is the word of God. If the Spirit wants to tell us things about Jesus and the wider plans of God, it makes sense to approach life armed with what he's told us.

Take up the sword of the Spirit.

That means making time to interact with the Bible. And not just here and there, on the fly. Not just the armpit of the day. Real time. Shut-the-door-and-switch-off-the-phone kind of time.

And it means approaching the Bible with humility. Not just looking for something to think about. Not just looking to be confirmed in what I already know. Real humility. I-thought-this-but-the-Bible-says-that-so-I'll-change-my-view kind of humility.

That's how to be truly Spiritual.

4

GOD'S KISS OF LIFE

IT was a long time ago. But I still remember the moment. It was the first time I'd seen a dead body with my own eyes.

I was already feeling pretty dazed before it happened. A sleepless overnight train ride into the city of Buenos Aires had left me well below par. Now I was jammed into a seat on a city bus, barely keeping my eyes open as the rough ride had me bobbing around.

It was a residential area. One of those long streets with cars parked tightly all the way along both sides of the road, and only really enough room for one car to head down the middle.

How the woman didn't see or hear us I will never know. The roar of the engine announced the bus's approach to the entire neighbourhood. But clearly she was unaware. She came out of nowhere. Out from behind a car, I guess aiming to cross the road. She never made it that far. The driver slammed the brakes on, but it was too late. She never stood a chance.

The bus stopped. There was confusion and loud talking. But eventually the passengers all filed off. And I just couldn't help myself. I stole a glance at the woman. Totally lifeless.

Not a spark or a glimmer of vitality in her.

It wasn't a marginal call. You didn't need a doctor to confirm it.

She was dead. It was plain to see.

She's the person I think of when I read Ephesians 2:1.

> As for you, you were dead in your transgressions and sins…

This is how my spiritual biography begins – and yours. We were spiritual corpses. *Not a spark or a glimmer of vitality.* That inert woman at the roadside in Buenos Aires is a picture of what you and I were.

It's a picture of anyone and everyone whose life is still dominated by 'the ways of this world', 'the ruler of the kingdom of the air', 'the cravings of the flesh' (verses 2-3). When the world, the flesh and the devil define your life, you're out of relationship with God. And out of relationship with God means spiritually dead.

It's what I was. But it's not what I am. That is not where my spiritual biography ends.

> But God, who is rich in mercy, made us alive with Christ even when we were dead in our transgressions… (verse 4).

God has breathed life into this corpse. Not just offered me a helping hand. Not just dosed me up with some kind of spiritual vitamins. No. More than that. He's given me the kiss of spiritual life.

We've seen already the four areas of God's fresh start that God is committed to bringing to his people by his Spirit. New speech, new power and new heart were three of them. But we're looking in this chapter at the most basic one of all: new life.

BORN AGAIN

You up for a bit of eavesdropping? Because that's what we're going to do now. We're about to listen in on a private conversation.

And I mean *private*. The man who initiated this conversation took great pains to make sure it was just that. he needed to.

Nicodemus was part of the top-tier Jewish leadership. So passing the time of day with an anti-establishment type like Jesus was not really an option for him – too much potential for comeback. He needed to watch his back.

So he doesn't pass the time of day with him. He comes by night instead. He wants to say to him in private what he could not say in public: he is seriously impressed by Jesus.

> You are a teacher who has come from God. Nobody could perform the signs you are doing if God were not with him (John 3:2).

I don't know what response from Jesus he's expecting here. 'Well, thank you very much'? 'Nice of you to say so'?

But I'm pretty sure he didn't anticipate what Jesus does in fact come back with.

> Very truly I tell you, no one can see the kingdom of God unless they are born again (verse 3).

Er. Right. OK.

It's fair to say Nicodemus is a bit wrong-footed by this comment from Jesus. He doesn't quite get what he's saying. But no matter, Jesus repeats himself and expands slightly.

> No one can enter the kingdom of God unless they are born of water and the Spirit (verse 5).

He's almost certainly referring not to water-baptism as we understand it, but to that prophecy in Ezekiel 36, which talks about how God will 'sprinkle clean water on you' and 'put my Spirit in you'.

But see how he goes on.

> Flesh gives birth to flesh, but the Spirit gives birth to spirit. You should not be surprised at my saying, 'You must be born again'. The wind blows wherever it pleases. You hear its sound, but cannot tell where it comes from or where it is going. So it is with everyone born of the Spirit (verses 6-8).

Jesus is saying at least three things here.

First, if you want to be part of God's kingdom, you're out of luck. Sorry, but it's just not going to happen – *not unless you experience new life.*

There are no coffins or graves in God's kingdom. There's nowhere to put spiritual corpses. New life is an essential entry requirement. 'You must be born again'.

Second, this new life is impossible to get. You just can't find it. Not even on Amazon. It's unattainable – *unless the Spirit of God is at work in you.*

You can't manufacture it. The only way you can get it is by receiving another dose of what gave Adam his life in the first place: the very breath of God. Nothing else will do the job. 'The Spirit gives birth to spirit.'

Third, you can't *make* the Spirit work in you. You can't get the Spirit to do the life-giving work you badly need. He will not give you that new birth – *unless he chooses to.*

That's presumably because you and I *can't* choose. Corpses don't take initiative. The initiative lies with the Spirit. 'The wind blows wherever it pleases.'

There's one big question, though, sitting there un-answered. What actually *is* this new life?

In a nutshell, the life the Spirit brings *is life in relationship with Jesus, on the basis of the death of Jesus.*

Jesus isn't finished yet with Nicodemus. He's an Old Testament expert. He should know his stuff when it comes to the experience of Israel during their forty years' wandering in the desert. So Jesus uses an illustration that he can relate to.

> Just as Moses lifted up the snake in the wilderness, so the Son of Man must be lifted up, that everyone who believes may have eternal life in him (verses 14-15).

Numbers 21 tells the story of Israel being attacked by a plague of snakes. For many of them, a snake bite was a death sentence. The clock started ticking on their lives as soon as they were bitten.

No way out.

Until God *did* provide a way out. He had Moses make a bronze snake on a pole: anyone bitten who looked at the bronze snake would live. Death sentence cancelled. Life assured.

As Jesus speaks to Nicodemus, he knows that he too, like that bronze snake of old, will be lifted up soon – on a cross. He also knows that this lifting up on the cross will be the basis on which others may find life. And he knows that the route to finding life will be to look to him. But there's yet another thing: the life that will be theirs when they do will be eternal life 'in him'.

It's even clearer in John 17. Jesus is in mid-prayer to his Father when he puts the matter beyond any doubt:

> Now this is eternal life: that they know you, the only true God, and Jesus Christ whom you have sent (John 17:3).

Many of us have somebody special in our lives. A close friend. A brother or sister. A husband or wife. Someone of whom we might say: 'I can't imagine life without him/her. In fact I'm not sure that life would be worth living without him/her.'

We're wrong, of course. Life is a gift from God and he does provide for us even when our 'special person' is wrenched away. But we still feel it sometimes.

It's different with the eternal life the Spirit gives us.

There really is no eternal life even possible except life in Jesus Christ.

In fact that's what eternal life means. We tend to define 'eternal life' by *quantity*: lots of life going on for lots of time, in fact for *all* time. But Jesus thinks of eternal life as defined in the first place by *quality*. It's a particular *kind* of life – life in relationship with him. That's the only kind of eternal life possible.

But there's good news: this is exactly the life the Spirit brings. He doesn't just bring Jesus Christ to the world. He works in the lives of individuals like you and me to bring us to Jesus Christ. To start trusting him. To start living for him. To start enjoying life with him.

BAPTISED IN THE SPIRIT?

The Bible has different ways of talking about the new life given to us by the Spirit. For example: receiving the

Spirit, the gift of the Spirit, being sealed in the Spirit, the Spirit coming on people. Or being baptised in the Spirit.

In each case the particular image is slightly different. But they're all describing the same thing at heart: God starting to work in someone at the beginning of their Christian life by his Spirit.

There's a problem, though. Some of the phrases have developed a bit of history. So they've become a bit confusing or even controversial. Baptism in the Spirit is one of them.

It's a repeated expression in the New Testament. It comes seven times: once in each gospel, twice in Acts and once in 1 Corinthians. All but one of them are references to what Jesus would do (or had done) as against John's baptism in water.

One thing about baptism in the Spirit that's abundantly clear is that it's something experienced by all Christians. You never come across a situation in the Bible where some have had it but not others. In fact, Paul is explicit about it being universal: 'We were all baptised by one Spirit' (1 Corinthians 12:13).

The point is: every Christian believer has been baptised in the Spirit!

But at the beginning of the twentieth century, a movement was born in Los Angeles called Pentecostalism. The USP (Unique Selling Point) of Pentecostalism was the offer of an experience like Pentecost for Christian believers today.

The logic went like this. 'The first disciples knew Jesus, but didn't experience the baptism of the Spirit until later, and when they did, the experience was very dramatic. So for us today, we can become Christians, but still not have been baptised in the Spirit. Baptism in the Spirit is something that comes later – sometime after conversion – and it comes with drama, especially speaking in tongues.'

The view has come to be known as 'second blessing theology' – for obvious reasons.

But should we expect a post-conversion, dramatic experience to be the norm for Christians today?

First things first. Make no mistake, it is what happened to some of the first believers. Particularly when the gospel first arrived at each of the new places on his programme.

At the start of Acts, Jesus talks about the Spirit in connection with three spheres of gospel witness.

'You will receive power when the Holy Spirit comes on you, and you will be my witnesses in Jerusalem, in Judea and Samaria, and to the ends of the earth' (Acts 1:8).

And when the Spirit first comes to each of those spheres, you can't miss the moment! Either the baptism in the spirit happens with a delay (i.e. it's separate from conversion) or it happens with drama (i.e. people start speaking in tongues) – or both. Either way, it's a big signpost: 'Look at this, everyone. The gospel is breaking new ground here! We're entering a totally new phase of witness!'

- In Acts 2, the Spirit comes to those in Jerusalem – and there's both the delay and the drama.

- In Act 8, the Spirit comes to those in Samaria – there's a delay, though not the drama.

- In Acts 10, the Spirit comes to those in the Gentile world, effectively the 'ends of the earth' – with no delay, but with the drama.

But that's it. After that first arrival in each of the three spheres, we never see anything like it again – no delay or drama – apart from one slightly odd 'time-warp' experience in Ephesus (Acts 19), when Paul comes across some disciples who've only had John's baptism. That's the lot.

The gospel goes to Antioch and Cyprus and Iconium and Lystra and Derbe and Philippi and Thessalonica and Berea and Athens – and all sorts of other places. And there's not a single mention of either the delay or the drama.

So it seems pretty clear what's going on. The delay (gap between conversion and the Spirit coming) and the drama (speaking in tongues) are connected specifically with the Spirit first going to those 3 new spheres, not normal Christian experience after that. We're still in that third phase (the mission to the Gentile world) now. That's the historical reality that Acts gives us.

In fact, as you read the New Testament, it becomes very obvious that to receive the Holy Spirit (or to be baptised with the Spirit – they both mean the same in the Bible) is the same thing as coming to Christ. So Paul says:

If anyone does not have the Spirit of Christ, they do not belong to Christ (Romans 8:9).

And again:

No one can say 'Jesus is Lord' except by the Holy
Spirit (1 Corinthians 12:3).

Just a few verses later, Paul says to every single Christian in Corinth: 'We were all baptised by one Spirit'
(1 Corinthians 12:13).

You can't be a Christian without having the Spirit.
So if you profess Christ as your Lord and Saviour, you
have received the baptism of the Spirit.

Why? Because it's the Spirit's work to bring us new
life – life in Jesus.

RESPONDING

Ballroom dancing has made a comeback recently. It's
fun to do, and great to watch – if you like that kind of
thing. Hence the TV ratings for watching celebrities have
a crack at it!

What's key is a good understanding between the part-
ners: one leads, the other follows. The one who follows is
not completely passive. Far from it. It's hard work doing
all that anticipating and adjusting. You've got to keep in
perfect step with your leader all the time. Not easy. But if
you get it right, it's beautiful to see.

Paul has an expression he uses about the way we interact with the Spirit of God. He says this: 'Since we live by the
Spirit, let us keep in step with the Spirit' (Galatians 5:25).

He's talking there specifically about holiness. But we
can broaden out the principle. At the end of each of these
chapters I want to ask you to think how best to respond to
what the Spirit has done and is doing in your life. What's
it going to look like to 'keep in step with the Spirit'?

In this chapter we've looked at the Spirit's work in
getting us going with Jesus in the first place. Getting us off

the starting blocks. Taking the spiritual corpses we were and giving us new life – life in Jesus, with Jesus. First by bringing Jesus to us, and then by bringing us to Jesus.

So how can we respond? Two suggestions:

1. Nurture an inner response of joy and thanksgiving.

When Paul wrote 'Rejoice in the Lord always' (Philippians 4:4), he was writing to seasoned believers. They needed to be reminded to keep nurturing their joy! Do you need the same reminder?

Everyone has something they get excited about. The score from their sports team at the weekend. The health of the roses in their garden. The reactions to their latest post on social media. The latest valuation of their stockmarket portfolio. The impressive accomplishments of their child. The upcoming new series of their favourite TV show. Fill in the blank for you. Everyone's got something that brings joy to their hearts.

But which of those things could be even in the same league as the new life you have in Christ? The truth is: nothing comes close. And yet when we think about where we now stand with God, does our heart start beating faster as it does with those other things?

Our joy index is totally out of kilter.

But wait a second. Isn't joy something you just feel? Isn't it something that just happens to you? You can't *make* yourself feel joyful, can you?

My daughter is an animal lover. She pestered us for years about having a pet. But we were unmoved. We figured we had a good idea of who would end up looking after a new member of the household! So we knocked her back. Every request, however earnestly made (or powerfully argued), got the same response.

One birthday, though, things changed. She'd worked her way through a nice little pile of presents and she came to the last one. It was not very exciting to look at – just an envelope with a card and a piece of paper inside. And the piece of paper wasn't even money. Not very promising. All a bit dull. And her face showed it.

But when she opened up the piece of paper and saw what it really was her face was transformed. It was a certificate (hastily knocked up on the computer!) which entitled the bearer to go and choose a kitten and bring it home.

The expression on her face was one of disbelief. She was over the moon. Grinning from ear to ear!

What made the change? Simple. She took time to read some words – words of promise, words that spoke of a precious gift. She needed to open it up, to look into what she had, and to realise the significance of it.

If you want to experience joy, that's the direction to head in. Don't look inside your heart and try to 'manufacture' something. Open your Bible. Read and reflect on the wonder of what God has done for you in Christ by the power of his Spirit. Feel the impact of it. Consider where you might have been had he not worked in that way. Ponder the differences between the spiritual corpse you were and the living believer you are now.

And you will find joy.

2. Keep looking to Jesus.

Remember the bronze snake? It was those who looked to the bronze snake who lived. And it's those who look to Jesus – believe in him, trust in him, orient their lives towards him – who experience eternal life.

How much does Jesus fill your thoughts? I mean, *really* fill your thoughts? What are some of the ways you express your dependence on him each day?

It's easy to let life just 'happen' to us, without thinking about the direction we're pointing our lives in, or to allow other people to fill our horizons. There are always people we'll want to please, or people we'll need to rely on, or people we think highly of. How about making sure Jesus is the one we ultimately want to please in the decisions we make. Making sure Jesus is the one we ultimately rely on to get us through our days. Making sure Jesus is the one we think the world of.

Reflect deeply on the beauty of his character. And keep looking to him.

5

SPEECH FOR THE TONGUE-TIED

IF you look at how internet usage has developed over the past couple of decades, one thing is obvious: images beat words hands-down.

They're the engine for social media. They provide the most popular entertainment. And they're a vital resource if you need to sell something: your product, or your political party, or the service you're offering.

Or even yourself. Imagine a dating website without pictures.

But for all that, words still have huge power. Think of these three words: 'I love you'.

Or another three words: 'It's a girl!'

Or how about just two: 'We won!'

Or else: 'I do.'

Whether we like it or not, words carry great force. They can do a load of good – or a load of harm.

The tongue has the power of life and death (Proverbs 18:21).

We know it from our own experience. We've all felt crushed at one time or another by something somebody has said. A few well-chosen words can destroy you.

But we've probably felt just the opposite too. That time when we had sunk as low as we could go, and that beautiful message arrived, or that card, or that text. It felt like we were brought up out of the pit.

The right words, at the right time, from the right person can change your life.

We've seen already that God is in the business of giving new speech to his people by his Spirit. He's been doing it since the days of Moses.

It's now time to see just what *form* that new speech takes.

We're now going to look in a bit more detail at how the Spirit helps Christian believers today to speak to God, to speak to each other and to speak to the world.

SPEAKING TO GOD

The gifts and blessings God pours out on his people are many. And they are extravagant. But the jewel in the crown is surely this: that he grants us a place at his family table. He has adopted us as his children!

This means some wonderful things. It means a glorious *inheritance*. At death we stand to gain the *full* experience of the greatest blessing imaginable: relationship with God himself. That's an inheritance of greater value than the biggest estate or the fattest cheque.

But as well as inheritance, being a child of God means access. We get to come into the presence of our Father

God right now. And we get to speak to him as members of his family.

That's what Paul is reflecting on in Romans 8:

> For those who are led by the Spirit of God are the children of God. The Spirit you received does not make you slaves, so that you live in fear again; rather the Spirit you received brought about your adoption to sonship. And by him we cry, 'Abba Father' (Romans 8:14-15).

This is almost beyond belief.

As followers of Jesus, we get to address God in exactly the same terms that Jesus himself does. Because of the Spirit, we get to call him 'Father': to talk to him, share our concerns with him, pour out our hearts to him.

All because of the Spirit.

Imagine a middle-aged couple at home one night. The house is quiet. Their boy is away at university. They're just debating how to spend their evening. They'll go out into the garden and water the roses, maybe grab a light dinner, enjoy a short walk before the sun sets, then watch the news before having an early night. How they look forward to seeing their boy again when he gets home.

The phone rings. There's lots of noise in the background, but they hear an unfamiliar voice say this: 'Hi there. I'm a bus driver. And I've got a football team on board my bus right now. They just had a big game and they're on the way home but the traffic is horrible. We're not going to make it back tonight. Is it OK to bring them to your house for a meal – just the fifteen of them – and maybe stay the night? We'll be there in an hour.'

What are our couple going to say?

Presumably something like: 'Er, no. I don't think so. I think you've probably got the wrong number. This is not a hotel. It's a home. And there's no way we're cooking for fifteen random people and letting them stay in our house. You must think we're crazy!'

But then the driver comes back to you. And he says:

'Oh sorry, I should have explained. The captain of our football team is your son Josh. I've got him here on the bus. He said you'd be happy to have him and his friends.'

What's their response now? How about:

'Got it. Pizza for fifteen coming up. It'll be ready in an hour. Everyone's welcome to bunk down tonight. If you're with Josh, then our home is your home. We'll look forward to hearing all about the day. Drive safely!'

Did you get the point?

The Spirit's the driver of the bus!

And if we're with Jesus, the Spirit takes us into the presence of the Father, and the Father will welcome us and treat us as part of the family and listen with interest to everything we've got to say – just as any parent would listen to their child.

Because of the Spirit, we get to speak and act as children of our heavenly Father.

In fact, it goes even further.

There are some families – maybe you've come across one – where one person often finishes off the sentences of another. Or else they'll rephrase what the other said, put it in a slightly different way. It can be either quite sweet or a bit irritating depending on your perspective.

That's more or less what the Spirit does for those of us in the family of Jesus, as we talk to our Father God.

When we talk to God, it turns out the Spirit is 'translating' what we pray to bring it in line with what God wants to hear!

> We do not know what we ought to pray for, but the Spirit himself intercedes for us through wordless groans (Romans 8:26).

(Just to be clear, 'wordless groans' is not referring to speaking in tongues: tongues is a gift only for some believers, but the whole of Romans 8 is about the experience of all believers.)

> And he who searches our hearts [that is, God the Father] knows the mind of the Spirit, because the Spirit intercedes for God's people in accordance with the will of God (verse 27).

It's hard to know exactly what's going on here. But the basic thrust is clear enough. The Spirit fills in for us in our prayers to God the Father. The Spirit communicates on our behalf. If we don't speak to our Father the things he wants to hear from us, the Spirit makes sure the Father hears the right things anyway!

PRAYING IN THE SPIRIT

Just because the Spirit 'fills in' for us, we still need to think about how we pray. The Spirit's work doesn't let us off the hook! That's why we need to be careful and deliberate about praying specifically 'in the Spirit' (Ephesians 6:18).

But what does that mean?

Some Christians think it means 'speak in tongues'. But it can't be that. True, there's a similar expression in 1 Corinthians 14 which is talking about tongues. But not this one. Here it is in context.

> [17] Take the helmet of salvation and the sword of the Spirit, which is the word of God.

> [18]And pray in the Spirit on all occasions with all kinds of prayers and requests. With this in mind, be alert and always keep on praying for all the Lord's people. [19]Pray also for me, that whenever I speak, words may be given me so that I will fearlessly make known the mystery of the gospel, [20]for which I am an ambassador in chains. Pray that I may declare it fearlessly, as I should.
>
> Straight away you can see that praying in the Spirit involves bringing different issues to God ('all kinds of prayers and requests'), which means it has to engage the mind. That automatically excludes speaking in tongues, which is a non-rational, non-mind-engaging type of prayer. In fact, Paul lists some of the specific issues he has in mind: for fellow Christians (verse 18), for his own word-choice (verse 19) and for his courage (verse 20). This is considered, rational prayer.
>
> Not tongues, then. So what is it? What's involved with praying in the Spirit?
>
> Look at the previous verse and it becomes clear. The encouragement there is to take God's word, which is called there the 'sword of the Spirit'. Since 'pray in the Spirit' comes straight afterwards, what's probably meant is: 'Make sure the word of God shapes your prayers'. Whatever you pray for, pray in a Bible way for it.

Speaking to each other.

There's an old children's illustration about how Christians should speak to each other. The teacher gets two children to have a race. Each gets a tube of toothpaste and the winner of the race is the one who gets all the toothpaste out of their tube first. And off they go.

When both have emptied their tubes, the teacher announces there's another stage to the race. 'OK, now you've got to get it all back in the tube. Are you ready? Go!'

Pretty soon, both children have given up, saying it's impossible. And the teacher says: 'You're right. It can't be done. And that's how it is with the words that come out of our mouths. What's said can never be unsaid. Think about that every time you open your mouth.'

It's pretty good as children's illustrations go. Actually it's not bad for an adult's illustration! It's a lesson we need to be reminded of frequently. But it only goes so far. It doesn't answer the question: 'What's wrong with speaking destructive words to a fellow-believer? Why does it matter?'

The answer is: it's working against what the Spirit is doing.

Part of the Spirit's work is to bring Christian believers together. See how the Spirit and the unity of God's people go together:

- 'For we were all baptised by one Spirit so as to form one body… and we were all given the one Spirit to drink' (1 Corinthians 12:13).

- 'And in [Christ] you too are being built together to become a dwelling in which God lives by his Spirit' (Ephesians 2:22).

A large part of expressing our unity as believers comes down to the way we talk to each other. Here are some fairly typical words from Paul. See if you can spot the connection between talking and the Spirit.

Do not let any unwholesome talk come out of your mouths, but only what is helpful for building others up according to their needs, that it may benefit those who listen. And do not grieve the Holy Spirit of God, with whom you were sealed for the day of redemption. Get rid of all bitterness, rage and anger, brawling and slander, along with every form of malice (Ephesians 4:29-31).

Our words to each other are to be wholesome and edifying; not bitter, angry or untruthful. The latter kind of talk is 'grieving the Spirit' – going against the grain of the Spirit's work. The former is in line with the Spirit.

So the Spirit is interested in bringing believers together through words of life. The Spirit is interested in truth rather than lies; in building up rather than tearing down; in nourishing rather than poisoning.

Speaking to the world

As we followed the story of the Spirit in the Old Testament we noticed that every now and again somebody was suddenly gripped by God's Spirit. It was temporary, but powerful. And it led to their speaking and acting in ways that made it very clear they were in the hold of a supernatural influence.

What's interesting is that in the New Testament, it still happens!

Even though every child of God has the Spirit, there are times when individuals are described as being specially 'filled with the Spirit'. Each time, the reason is the same: they're filled with the Spirit in order to be able to speak of Christ boldly to unbelieving people.

In Acts 4 Peter is arrested after performing a healing. The leaders quiz him about what's really going on: 'By what power or what name do you do this?'

And then out it comes.

Then Peter, filled with the Holy Spirit, said to them, '… know this, you and all the people of Israel: it is by the name of Jesus Christ of Nazareth, whom you crucified but whom God raised from the dead, that this man stands before you healed' (Acts 4:8-10).

It's not just the fact that he spoke, though. Or even what he said (though that's key). It's how he spoke that they pick up on:

When they saw the courage of Peter and John… (verse 13).

Being filled with the Spirit has helped them to speak courageously for Christ.

It happens again at the prayer meeting shortly afterwards:

… they were all filled with the Holy Spirit and spoke the word of God boldly (Acts 4:31).

Are you spotting a pattern?

It's there again with Stephen in chapter 7. And Paul in chapter 13.

You can't miss it. When we speak with particular courage – or perhaps with particular aptness or wisdom – that's the Holy Spirit coming upon us in a particular way in order to point others towards Jesus.

'Filled with the Spirit'?

We've seen that being filled with the Spirit is linked to speaking about Christ, i.e. evangelism. But is that all? What about when unusual or supernatural things start happening? Or when there's someone who seems to have an uncanny kind of insight into people? Or there's an atmosphere – maybe after a 'time of worship' – that just sends tingles down your spine? Don't those gatherings or individuals merit a label of 'filled with the Spirit'?

There is actually one other time when this kind of language is used. And this time it's a command.

> Do not get drunk on wine, which leads to debauchery. Instead be filled with the Spirit (Ephesians 5:18).

Preachers love an image to play with – and then push the image to the limits. I know, I am one. (A preacher, that is.) So it's hardly surprising when you hear a preacher talking about *how* full of the Spirit we are, and then milking the image: 'We leak. We need to fill up.' It sounds almost like pulling the car over to top up whatever's in the tank.

It's a nice picture. But it's bad Bible-reading. Sloppy. Read the verse carefully and you see the contrast is not between being *filled* with the Spirit and being *empty* of the Spirit (or even half-full). The contrast is between (a) being filled with the *Spirit* and (b) being drunk on *wine*. In other words, *it's about who or what is the controlling influence in our lives* (wine or the Spirit) and what is the behaviour that will result (debauchery or what he describes in verses 19-21).

Be filled with the Spirit. That means: act towards God and towards your fellow believers in such way as to demonstrate God is in charge of your life!

It's not about the *feeling* in some gathering or about the *aura* given off by some individual.

It is about encouraging each other with God-focussed words (verse 19), worshipping God and saying thank you to him in our hearts (verses 19-20), and submitting to each other as we should (verse 21).

So if you long to be 'Spirit-filled' in this sense, aim to behave towards God and others like this.

SO SPEAK UP

The invention of the telephone surely ranks among the top ten technological achievements of all time. I don't profess to understand how it actually works; if I were among a small group of survivors of some nuclear holocaust, the task of reinventing it would have to fall to someone other than me.

But it is truly a thing of wonder. When I look at that little gadget in my hand, and ponder the inventing genius of Alexander Graham Bell, the technological contributions of countless other individuals, the financial investment of corporations and governments down the years, the aesthetic improvements of others and so on – I'm overwhelmed. The amount of intellectual and practical firepower that's gone into enabling me to speak to people across the planet is mindboggling.

If I want to honour this great tool, I could go about it in different ways. For example, I could install it in an airtight glass case and display it as an artefact on the mantelpiece in my living room. Every time I or anyone else enters that room, we might see it and wonder at it, open-mouthed and speechless in admiration.

Or I could just use it. Keep it charged. And make the calls it was designed to enable.

Which of those approaches seems a more appropriate way to you?

God's Spirit has been at work for thousands of years to enable us to communicate. He's been taking care of all the blockages and challenges to make it possible for us to speak to God, to other members of our spiritual families, and to the world at large.

And our response is… what? Just to marvel at this great work? Remain open-mouthed and speechless in wonder at how amazing the Spirit is?

I don't think so.

There has to be a better response.

How about this:

1. Speak long, often and intentionally to your heavenly Father in prayer.

God the Father made people to relate to him. God the Son made it possible for people to relate to the Father. And God the Spirit has applied that possibility to *you*, if you know Jesus. You can come into the Father's presence at any time. You can pull up a chair to his family dinner table and call him 'Abba, Father'. You can pray!

So why not be intentional about it? By all means go about your daily life talking to God here and there on the way through. But in practice that often means giving him the fag-end of your attention: talking to him, generally a bit superficially, when there's nothing more pressing to occupy your attention.

How about making sure there's at least one point every day where can have a sustained talk with him. And consider putting some structure into that time, so that you don't just default to the same kind of prayers.

If we're to pray 'in the Spirit', we'll need God's Spirit-inspired Word to set the agenda. For example:

- Use each line of the Lord's prayer
  (Matthew 6:9-13) as a basis for your own
  prayers

- Riff on the prayers of Paul, so that they set your basic prayer themes, but you make them your own

- Pick up the old acronym 'ACTS' so that your prayers include an element of adoration, confession, thanksgiving and supplication

However you do it, make sure you're speaking to your Father the kind of things he wants to hear. But remember: you don't have to be a pro. The Spirit will make sure every prayer you pray reaches the Father's ear the way it should!

2. Speak words of life to your fellow-believers, not words of death.

Have you ever noticed all those 'one another' instructions in the New Testament? Among other things, we who are part of the community of the Spirit are encouraged to:

- love one another (John 13:34)

- be devoted to one another (Romans 12:10)

- accept one another (Romans 15:7)

- agree with one another (1 Corinthians 1:10)

- greet one another (2 Corinthians 13:12)

- serve one another (Galatians 5:13)

- bear with one another (Ephesians 4:2)

- forgive one another (Ephesians 4:32)

- teach and admonish one another (Colossians 3:16)

- build one another up (1 Thessalonians 5:11)

- encourage one another (Hebrews 3:13)

- spur one another on (Hebrews 10:24)

- live in harmony with one another (1 Peter 3:8)

- offer hospitality to one another (1 Peter 4:9)

- have fellowship with one another (1 John 1:7)

A lot of those require practical expressions of love. But they nearly all require words.

A Spirit community is a speaking community.

For many of us, our communication with each other is dominated by putting across information or plans, sharing news and gossip about other people, or getting things off our chests. But look through that list above. How much of those things do you see?

3. Speak the truth about Jesus with courage and sensitivity to those who need to hear it

Time is short. Right now, Jesus is delaying his return so that more people can have opportunity to respond to his saving gospel.

And the Spirit is making sure that opportunity is real. He's set out the message to be spoken. He's preparing the hearts of those who will hear that message. And he's supplying the circumstances and contexts for the message to be spoken, as well as the courage needed for us to step up to the occasion and get on with the speaking.

The only question remaining is: will we, in fact, speak?

Not everyone is gifted as an Evangelist (with a capital E). But most of us can find ways to drop words in our daily conversations with others that might lead to their encountering the gospel. If we get tongue-tied, we can offer a leaflet, give an invitation to a course or event, introduce them to a more spiritually articulate friend and so on.

But remember: those who find new life often do so on the basis of the most stumbling attempts to articulate the gospel – because those attempts were backed with the credibility of a consistent, God-honouring, Spirit-enabled lifestyle.

So take courage. Speak up as you have opportunity. And experience the joy of the Spirit using you to draw others to Jesus.

6

POWER TO THE PEOPLE

NEW life and new speech are all very well. But if there's one thing the Holy Spirit is famous for in the Christian world, it's his works of *power*. Obvious, undeniable displays of raw, divine power.

The sort of power that miraculously heals people of lifelong diseases. Or kicks out demons from a person's life. Or dramatically reveals impossible-to-guess secrets to somebody. Or takes obvious control of an entire roomful of believers. Maybe even raises the odd person from the dead.

Mention the Spirit, and most Christians will think of instances like these. These moments of – you know – weirdness! When the laws of nature are temporarily put on hold, and an outside force – God himself – takes charge.

It's moments like these when you *really* see God at work. Or so we've been taught to believe.

We've been taught wrongly.

Here's the problem with that way of thinking: *it just makes God too small.*

GOD AT WORK

The Bible's picture of God is of a 24/7 worker. He's busy all the time. He's constantly got his hands full, running the world from second to second. Like the conductor of an orchestra tackling a great symphony, the job God has set himself is to keep everything on track all the way to the final chord.

But that's not how we've come to see him.

The BBC Proms is billed as the greatest classical music festival on earth. Every day for two months, the people of Britain pile into the Royal Albert Hall or the Cadogan Hall. A third of a million people attend in person. Sixteen million people watch one or more concerts on TV. And yes, this is for classical music!

To see the conductor standing before a great orchestra there in the Royal Albert Hall, giving the beat for all the players from start to finish, keeping the whole show on the road, is to see a picture of God. It is God who sustains the world from moment to moment. He provides the life force for the whole operation. Were he to put his baton down, the thing would fall apart.

But there's somebody else on view at a BBC Prom. High up over the orchestra, looking down from on high, surveying the scene, is the bust of Sir Henry Wood.

Sir Henry Wood was the founding conductor of the Proms. It was he who designed the series, gave it its demo-cratic ethos, turned it into reality back in 1895. By having his bust on display at every concert, the organisers of the Proms are making a very clear statement: this man is the reason we're all here!

Over the last century or so, more and more Christians around the world have been influenced by a worldview called 'deism'. Deism presents God as not personally involving himself in the day-to-day operations of the world. His main contribution was to get the cosmos going. To flick the first domino. Now that everything's up and running, his work is finished. So he just leaves it be.

You could call it the 'Sir Henry Wood' version of God. Sitting up there on high, looking down on his creation, but retired from active service. The symphony is written. The performance has started. The players can take care of themselves.

As I say, Christians around the world have started to see God a bit like this. Science seems to have an explanation for almost everything. So why do you need 'God' to explain normal life? You don't!

And so we no longer really believe that God is responsible for keeping the universe going from moment to moment.

But God has to do *something*! He has to interact with the world in *some* way. So this is the role we assign to him: when something happens that we don't understand and science can't easily explain, *that's* God at work. Every now and then, the 'Sir Henry Wood' God comes to life and jumps down from his perch to put something right. He's an occasional interferer. He 'tinkers'.

And when God tinkers, it's always impressive. Miraculous, we'd call it. Signs, wonders, astonishing experiences. Things that are worth talking up and getting excited about! And because there are obvious associations with power, we see these tinkerings as the Holy Spirit's department.

But after the tinkering's done, God's out of there. Back to his perch. Where he then remains until the next outing.

We're left waiting – and maybe praying – for an effectively absentee God to get to work again.

Do you see what's happened? We've taken God out of the 'ordinary' things. Out of the 'little' things. We've forgotten those words of Jesus:

> Are not two sparrows sold for a penny? Yet not one of them will fall to the ground outside your Father's care (Matthew 10:29).

And we've forgotten those words of Paul:

> God 'works out all things in conformity with the purpose of his will' (Ephesians 1:11).

In limiting God to the occasional and the extraordinary and the spectacular, we've shrunk him down. We've made him smaller. And specifically, we've made the Spirit smaller.

If you want to think more about this God-shrinkage and how it affects our daily walk with God, for example our prayer lives, our reaction to suffering, our approach to decision-making and evangelism, then you might want to get hold of my previous book, *Big God*.

But with that caution in mind, let's get back to the ways God works in power by his Spirit.

We've already seen a number of these ways. We've thought about:

> ➤ The power of the Spirit in conquering ignorance and bringing the knowledge of God,

> ➤ The power of the Spirit in breaking the power of death to raise spiritual corpses to life,

> The power of the Spirit in overcoming cowardice so that people can speak about God in courage – among others.

In this chapter we're going to focus on one particular display area: the Spirit's empowering of Christians to serve. Or as it's more commonly referred to, 'spiritual gifts' – 'gifts of the Spirit'.

GIFTS OF THE SPIRIT

The phrase 'gifts of the Spirit' or 'spiritual gifts' is actually not a biblical one. There's the singular ('spiritual gift') in Romans 1:11. And there's the word 'spirituals' (which some versions *paraphrase* as 'spiritual gifts' because of the context) in 1 Corinthians 12:1 and 14:1. But no 'gifts of the Spirit' in the Bible.

That said, there are gifts, and they are distributed by the Spirit. And we might summarise what the Bible says about them in three statements.

THE SPIRIT EMPOWERS ALL BELIEVERS WITH THESE GIFTS

The first part of the twentieth century, as we saw in chapter 4, saw the rise of the Pentecostals. They're still around today – and in large numbers. But later in the twentieth century, in the 60s and 70s, another movement emerged. The Charismatic movement.

Unlike the Pentecostals, they didn't prioritise starting new denominations. Many churches were started, and indeed some charismatic denominations, but most stayed in their existing churches to influence them, at least to start with. And one of the many positive ways that influence was felt was in a renewed appreciation for the gifts of God's Spirit today.

Many churches believed the Spirit's gifts were only for the apostles. Or maybe the apostles plus the first generation of Christians. Not for our generation.

Others thought the gifts were only for a few key players in church life, not for everyone else. Or if they didn't actually think so, they certainly behaved as though they did!

But the charismatic challenge (and, by the way, *charismata* just means 'gifts') was: 'No, the gifts are for everyone!' It was a real power-to-the-people thing. Literally.

And it was completely in line with the New Testament. So Paul writes:

> Now to each one the manifestation of the Spirit is given for the common good (1 Corinthians 12:7).

After listing a few specific gifts, he repeats himself:

> All these are the work of one and the same Spirit, and he distributes them to each one, just as he determines (verse 11).

Thanks to God's generosity and the power of his Spirit, every believer has a gift or gifts. However ungifted you or I might *feel*, if we're Christian believers we have gifts.

This realisation, though, brings with it a danger. It's that we start focussing on ourselves. Either we worry: 'What's my gift? Do I really have one? It can't be much needed!' Or we go to the other extreme: 'Look at my gift – aren't I special?!'

So we need to get this second point.

THE GIFTS ARE FOR SERVING THE CHURCH, NOT MYSELF

The point is made repeatedly. Gifts are given 'for the common good' (1 Corinthians 12:7). They are given 'so that the church may be edified' (14:5) – that is, built up. In

Romans 1:11, Paul says he wants to impart some spiritual gift 'to make you strong'.

They're all different ways of saying the same thing: any gift or gifts I've been given are not about me, they're about those around me.

Once we really get this, the whole question of identifying your gifts becomes a whole lot easier. In years gone by, the notorious 'gift inventory' (a bit like a personality profile test) was popular. It's probably been replaced by an app now. Don't get me wrong, these kind of approaches can be useful. They might help start a conversation, but they're also fraught with dangers.

When somebody at the church I serve says to me, 'Orlando, I'm not sure what my gift is', my response will be something along the lines of: 'Well, start by praying for wisdom and discernment. Then have a look around and see what needs doing. See if you're in a position to help. Ask others if they think you'd be a good fit for the role. If you are, that's your gift. Go and grow into it.'

But if they were to say, 'Orlando, I've got this gift – I need some context in which to put it to use', then they've likely missed the point. It's not about you or me and what we've got. It's about the church family and what they need.

In fact, it's possibly not too much to say that the second approach is just putting a Christian top hat on to worldly individualism and self-fulfilment. 'I need to express who I am' is the message. It's an attitude that has little to do with the gifts of the Spirit.

And that's why Paul is relatively down on the gift of tongues *in church*. The gift of tongues (or *glossolalia* to give it its proper name) is a way of speaking without full and conscious control of what you're saying. It's not a distinctly Christian thing – it's something people in other religions do. But Paul did it, he says he'd like others to do it, and lots of people do find it helpful.

The point he makes repeatedly, though, in 1 Corinthians 14 is that it's not at the top of the list as far as gifts go.

> Since you are eager for gifts of the Spirit, try to excel in those that build up the church (verse 12).

Or again:

> ...in the church I would rather speak five intelligible words to instruct others than 10,000 words in a tongue (verse 19).

In other words: unless you can harness your gift of tongues for others, like find someone to 'translate' what you're saying so we can all understand it, then best leave it at home!

It's become normal in many circles to ignore the Bible at this point, despite how clear it is. There's a feeling that if you see people speaking in tongues at a Christian meeting, it's a mark of the Spirit. The truth is, if people are speaking in tongues in a Christian meeting, it's usually a sign of the Spirit being *ignored or defied* – unless the tongues are interpreted.

Because it's not about me. It's all about the other person.

That's why 'prophecy' is such a positive gift for Paul in the context of a church gathering – and should be for us. Churches, of course, 'do' prophecy in different ways. If prophecy is – as it seems to be in the New Testament – simply some kind of informal and non-authoritative bringing of the word of God to bear on the lives and situations of others in church (or the church as a whole), then it's hardly surprising that different church cultures reflect this differently.

In our church, we experience prophecy in a number of contexts.

- Scores of people meet up regularly with someone a little younger in the faith than them. They meet generally with the *Bible* open, but also with their *ears* open to the specifics of that young believer's life. And they seek to help that person discern the voice of God for them: his encouragements, his challenges, his instructions.

- Nearly all meet in small groups, where members seek, again with Bibles open, to play their part in bringing God's word to each other.

- And our Sunday evening gathering normally includes a time for questions, comments and prophetic insights once we've carefully engaged with the Bible.

In all these contexts, some will often speak more than others. Perhaps they are the ones with a particular *gift* of prophecy. But others will contribute too, as you'd expect from believers living in an age where all prophesy.

That's how it works out in our church. Other churches might have a different culture or value different things (e.g. spontaneity or drama or abstract images). The key thing is serving others (rather than self) by speaking God's word into their life or lives.

And that leads us to the third statement.

THE GIFTS ARE DIVERSE, NOT LIMITED

Sometimes when you hear people talk about 'spiritual gifts', it turns out the only ones they're really interested in are the ones with the 'wow' factor: speaking in tongues, prophecy, healing, miracles.

The reason for that is what we saw at the start of this chapter: we've bought into the 'Sir Henry Wood' view of God. In our minds, we've removed God from the ordinary, day-to-day running of his world. We've shrunk God down. Sent him into retirement. All that's really left of him are the things we can't otherwise explain.

The truth is, though, the gifts include a much larger number of relatively 'ordinary'-looking activities. In fact, larger than any of the lists of gifts given to us in the New Testament.

The most famous gift-list is probably the one in 1 Corinthians 12:8-11. There are a total of nine gifts listed there. But it would be foolish to think of that as an exhaustive list. Apart from anything else, there's another list in verse 28 of the same chapter. Of the seven items there, there's some overlap with the earlier one, but also some new entries. And then there's the list in Romans 12:6-8 – another 7 gifts, some of them mentioned in 1 Corinthians 12, but most not. Oh, and another one in Ephesians 4:11. And yet another – albeit a little on the short side – in 1 Peter 4:11.

Look at these various lists, and one thing becomes very obvious: none of them is exhaustive. They're all context-specific. There's not some kind of definitive list, itemising all the possibilities for what your gift or mine could be.

The Christian community of which you are part will determine the gifts the Spirit gives. In the church I serve, there are a large number of university students who are with us for around 30 weeks of the year, but back home with their parents for the remaining time. Their church at home is often a very different community with very different needs to their church in their university city.

So inevitably those who serve in both contexts often find they are asked to exercise very different gifts. They might be exercising the gift of website design at home (because even though it's not really their thing, there are few others with even the most basic skills in that area). Or the gift of cleaning (because the annual church spring clean tends to happen when they're back home). Whereas at uni, they're exercising the gift of child-care (because we've had a baby spree lately). Or the gift of welcoming (because we tend to have a large number of new people with us every Sunday).

Suppose your church is planning a church plant to meet in a school and your church leaders ask you to take on the role of liaising with the school caretaker for Sunday access. What's your response? You could say: 'I'm sorry, but I've checked 1 Corinthians 12, Romans 12, Ephesians 4 and 1 Peter 4, and there's no gift of caretaker-liaison, so I'm afraid I can't help' – your leaders are not likely to be impressed with that!

Here's the point: the gifts you can expect the Spirit to equip you for will be determined by the context at least as much as your abilities, or indeed the contexts of the New Testament churches.

Most of the gifts are very ordinary, not obviously 'supernatural'. And – more than that – they're to be exercised in normal ways.

When a guitarist steps up to help with music at our Sunday gatherings, are we looking to her to break the laws of harmony and rhythm? No we are not! There will be more evidence of the Spirit working when she practises hard to conform to musical conventions than when she goes off on one.

It's the same when a new guy joins the finance team. Are we looking to him to break the laws of mathematics and accounting? No we are not. If he's truly exercising a gift given by the Spirit, he'll work with the normal expectations of the bank, the Charity Commission, the tax office, and indeed the church leadership.

Because the gifts are all about serving other people, they're largely very *ordinary* activities and are exercised in very ordinary ways. But they are as *diverse* as the needs other people may have.

'SIGNS AND WONDERS': DRAMATIC AND MIRACULOUS INTERVENTIONS OF THE SPIRIT

In the section above, we focussed on the *ordinariness* of most of the gifts of the Spirit. But what about the *extraordinary* and the inexplicable? What about the Holy Spirit and signs and wonders? Words of knowledge, healings, dramatic divine interventions in history. Should we expect to see such obvious displays of power on show as routinely as they seem to have been in Bible times?

Let me attempt a careful answer to that which runs with the contours of the Bible.

1. Signs and wonders are not routine in the Bible.
It may seem at first glance like there are stupendous displays of raw divine power on almost every page. But look carefully and you'll see there are only four periods of intense activity in terms of signs and wonders.

    i.   Around the time of the Exodus (around 1400 B.C.), for about fifty years – from the burning bush to the conquest of the promised land. Then – nothing for hundreds of years.

ii. In the time of Elijah and Elisha (around 850 B.C.) Then – nothing for a couple of hundred years.

iii. In the life of Daniel (around 600 B.C.). Then – nothing recorded for 500 years.

iv. During the time of Jesus and the apostles (1st century A.D.).

For most of the history covered by the Bible, there was precious little dramatic miracle activity – except for miracles of judgement, like the Flood (Genesis 5-10), or Sodom and Gomorrah (Genesis 19), or Uzziah being struck with leprosy for contempt towards the temple (2 Chronicles 26). During most of the Bible times, it was all quiet on the 'signs and wonders' front. Everything just happened by God running history through ordinary sequences of cause and effect.

2. Dramatic miracles started disappearing very quickly after Pentecost.
There was drama all around in the birth and adult ministry of Jesus, and in the early ministry of the apostles. But quite soon, even for key Christian leaders, unhealed sickness and disease became the norm.

- In 1 Corinthians, for example, there's much talk of the gift of healing. But by 2 Corinthians Paul has got his 'thorn in the flesh' which God isn't taking away, even though Paul pleads with God about it (12:8). There is no healing in view.

- In Philippians, Epaphroditus is very ill, but there's no miraculous healing spoken of there either. When God does eventually heal him, it doesn't seem to be through anything dramatic (2:27).

- In 1 Timothy, Timothy – one of the key players in the early church – apparently has a stomach disorder: he has 'frequent illnesses'. But again, in addressing him, Paul doesn't talk of looking for dramatic healing; he simply suggests trying to keep it under control by a bit of wine for medicinal purposes (5:23).

Spot the contrast? There's no big deal made of it, but the apostles do seem to sense that the period of frequent signs and wonders is over. Which makes sense: one of the key purposes of signs and wonders in the Bible was to authenticate a particular person or their message; once that work was done (especially as the books of the Bible came to be written), there's not such a need for that.

But there's something else too. With such a great and powerful God on our side, it's tempting to aspire to 'power' and 'victory' and 'conquering': stamping out the stains of sin all around us in the world. Many churches today use such language. 'Power this'. 'Victory that'.

But that wasn't how the New Testament writers thought, spoke and wrote. Paul repeatedly delighted, even boasted, in weakness (e.g. 2 Corinthians 11-12). Peter spoke of restoration and strength coming only *when we enter glory* (1 Peter 5:10). The writer to the Hebrews insisted on *enduring hardship as discipline* (Hebrews 12:7). James wrote of the 'joy' of facing trials (James 1:2). John's description of victory looked like *persevering, enduring hardship and not growing weary* (Revelation 2:3).

We are spiritual conquerors. The future is bright. There is joy (and even some measure of victory) available to us even today. But the hallmarks of the Christian life in the here and now include physical suffering, weakness and trials, from which we're not encouraged to expect lasting relief this side of the return of Jesus.

3. God does heal today, but normally through medical processes

Clearly God does heal in inexplicable ways. Ways that defy the understanding or expectations of doctors. What we usually refer to as a 'miracle'. Churches across the planet see this time and time again. I certainly have, a number of times.

But much more often, he does it through people, say, taking antihistamines, or going through months of physio or having their appendix removed. Medication, rehab, surgery – that kind of thing. For those with a small view of God, this may seem unimpressive: aren't these are just 'natural' or 'human' processes? But for those with a big view of God, this reality will be incredibly exciting: it's a reminder that God has every process of the universe in his hands, and he's using those processes to heal millions of people every day.

So yes, God heals and he may do it dramatically. If he does, rejoice. But don't expect it. And don't rejoice any less if he chooses to heal in more mundane-seeming ways.

RESPONDING

Every day, you and I as Christian believers have to make a decision: will I go with what God is doing by his powerful Spirit? Or will I get in his way?

There's no doubt that the Spirit is powerful. That's how the apostles were encouraged to think of him right at the start. Remember the words of the risen Jesus to the eleven:

…you will receive power when the Holy Spirit comes on you… (Acts 1:8).

But there's equally no doubt that people can and do try to get in the way of that power being exercised.

- Referring to the Spirit's work of building up the Christian community, Paul warns the Ephesians not to 'grieve the Holy Spirit of God' by destructive words towards fellow members of their community (Ephesians 4:30).

- Referring to the Spirit's work of revealing God's will through the Old Testament prophets, Stephen complains to the Jerusalem leadership: 'you always resist the Holy Spirit' by rejecting those sent by God (Acts 7:51).

- Referring to the Spirit's work of revealing God's will through his spokespersons today, the Thessalonians receive a caution: 'Do not quench the Spirit' (1 Thessalonians 5:19).

Grieving the Spirit. Resisting the Spirit. Quenching the Spirit. Three expressions to say much the same thing: getting in the way of the work of God's powerful Spirit.

As we consider what it might look like to do that, and how to avoid it, let me suggest three questions to reflect on.

1. In terms of my place in my Christian community, am I a genuine participant – or just a consumer?

Life is busy. There are so many calls on our time and energy. There's work, family, friends, leisure pursuits, emails, community activities, personal admin, shopping, TV and books, house maintenance, other projects. And when all those things are done, we need to sleep!

That's a lot of stuff going on. It's hard to think of how we could prioritise any real involvement with church. It's alright for some people. They just don't seem to have as much in their lives. But I do. I'll try to get along to Sunday church, and maybe something else in the week when I can. But beyond that, I can't be really expected to put more in. Not at this stage of my life. Right?

Wrong.

It was Jesus himself who showed us what serving looked like. It involved death to self for the benefit of others.

> For even the Son of Man came not to be served, but to serve, and to give his life as a ransom for many (Mark 10:45).

And now the Spirit Jesus sent equips every believer with what he or she needs – specifically to serve others and build up the church of which they are part.

Church is not a spectator sport. If we want to work with the Spirit, we need to get off the sidelines and on to the field.

2. When it comes to my activity in my church community, am I doing it to serve others, or is it in all honesty myself that I am serving?

Most of us are masters of self-deception. So it's hard to know our true motivations.

- Am I doing this to relieve a sense of guilt?

- Or because it's easier than saying 'no' for a people-pleaser like me?

- Or because I'm looking for an opportunity to show off an impressive talent?

- Or because I think it will win me points with God?

- Or just to keep myself busy?

In reality, our motivations are always mixed. If we wait for a pure heart before getting stuck in, we'll be waiting a long time.

But it is still worth seeking to work with the Spirit at the level of our motivations.

> Now to each one the manifestation of the Spirit is given for the common good (1 Corinthians 12:7).

Next time you undertake some work of service in your church community, why not ask God first that he would use that service first and foremost so that he or she – or indeed the church as a whole – might be built up.

And if you've been undertaking a role for a while, ask God for wisdom and clarity to see whether others really are being served more than you!

3. In terms of my ability to recognise the power of the Spirit, is my vision big or small?

Remember what the Spirit is about. The Spirit is God's agent to perform God's work in God's world. What God does in and around us – and he does *a lot* – he does by his Spirit.

And we need to learn to see things in that light.

When you use a UV lamp to survey a scene, anything that's white is highlighted. So switch it on and you'll likely see mostly darkness, but occasional spots of light. Many Christians see the power of the Spirit like that. Only where the unexpected happens do we recognise the work of the Spirit.

We need a better lamp.

The power of the Spirit is all around us. There may be different shapes in view, but it's all light.

So do rejoice when you see God's work in dramatic and inexplicable ways. Thank God. Sing out his praise. But don't sing any more quietly when good things happen slowly, gradually, or 'naturally'. Because the Spirit works just as much through the processes of nature as when those processes are breached.

7

HEART TRANSPLANTS FOR ALL

CLEAR eyes. Full hearts. Can't lose.

That line has been used as a strapline for more than one political campaign, and as a mantra for facing personal struggles in life. But it started life as a motivational line used by Coach Eric Taylor in the television drama 'Friday Night Lights'. It was repeated each week by the football team at the centre of the drama, as the players went out to battle yet another adversary on the field.

Clear eyes. Make sure at all times that you can see without distraction who and what lies ahead of you, as well as being aware of your own position on the field.

Full hearts. Let your personal performance – and indeed your team performance – flow from hearts that are bursting with yearning and desire.

Can't lose. Whatever the scoreboard may say now, have no doubt that the final result is not in doubt. Victory is assured.

As inspiring one-liners go, it's rarely been bettered.

Surprisingly enough, it's also not bad as a summary for the final great work of the Spirit to which we now turn.

Clear eyes. Full hearts. Can't lose.

CLEAR EYES

Your school biology textbook may have said otherwise, but the apostle Paul is clear on one thing: the human heart has eyes.

> I pray that the eyes of your heart may be enlightened…
> (Ephesians 1:18).

What does he mean? Simply that he is looking to God – and specifically, as it turns out, the work of God's Spirit – to enable the Christian believers to whom he writes to see more clearly.

What is it they need to see so clearly? Nothing less than the future God has mapped out for them.

Have a look at that little extract in context.

> When you believed, you were marked in him [i.e. Christ] with a seal, the promised Holy Spirit, who is a deposit, guaranteeing our inheritance until the redemption of those who are God's possession – to the praise of his glory.
>
> For this reason, ever since I heard about your faith in the Lord Jesus and your love for all God's people, I have not stopped giving thanks for you, remembering you in my prayers. I keep asking that the God of our Lord Jesus Christ, the glorious Father, may give you the Spirit of wisdom and revelation, so that you may

know him better. I pray that the eyes of your heart may be enlightened, in order that you may know the hope to which he has called you, the riches of his glorious inheritance in his holy people (Ephesians 1:13-18).

In the Bible, the 'heart' isn't just the HQ for your emotional life. It's the centre of your whole being: your thoughts, attitudes and decisions. So for the believer's 'heart' to be focussed on the hope to which they've been called is for their whole life to be zeroing in on that hope.

And that's what all genuine Christian believers do. Hope is part of our spiritual DNA.

As Peter puts it, the new birth that God gives us as we begin the Christian life is by its very nature:

a new birth into a living hope… and into an inheritance that can never perish, spoil or fade (1 Peter 1:3-4).

But here's the thing. If and when we are in fact gripped by that hope, it will be as a result of the work of God's Spirit in us. That's Paul's logic in that passage from Ephesians 1 quoted above. And it's just the same elsewhere:

Through the Spirit, by faith, we ourselves eagerly await the hope of righteousness (Galatians 5:5).

May the God of hope fill you with all joy and peace in believing, so that by the power of the Holy Spirit you may abound in hope (Romans 15:13).

You can't miss it. It is a key part of the work of God's Spirit to draw our attention and focus – the 'eyes of our hearts' – to the future we have with Jesus.

To help us understand exactly how the Spirit achieves this, Paul uses three simple illustrations.

➢ The Spirit is a 'seal' marking us out for God's future claim.

This is the picture in view at the start of that longer extract above. Here it is again:

> When you believed, you were marked in him [i.e. Christ] with a seal, the promised Holy Spirit (Ephesians 1:13).

A seal is (or at least was) a form of ID. It was a unique identifying mark on an animal that you owned, or some other possession. It did the job of a nametag. It was how an owner said: 'the one who wears this is *mine and mine alone'*.

And the point of it was to enable the owner to come back one day and claim what was theirs. You wouldn't bother to attach a seal to your property if you weren't coming for it someday. So if you did go to the trouble, you were communicating something very strongly: 'I'm coming back for you, so hang in there.'

Years ago, I did some short-term missionary work in Peru. But before I got on the plane, I put a ring on the finger of the girl I loved. It was my version of a seal. It was my saying to anyone who needed to hear it: 'hands off – she's mine (and I'm hers). I'm coming back for her.'

And yes. Before you ask, I did!

That is what the Spirit is for us – God's seal; his assurance that he's going to come and claim us soon.

➢ The Spirit is the 'firstfruits' of God's harvest to come.

In Romans 8 Paul talks about what it's like to be at this particular point in God's plans. Listen to his description:

> …we ourselves, who have the firstfruits of the Spirit, groan inwardly as we wait for our adoption, the redemption of our bodies… (Romans 8:23).

In other words, the *full* experience of being drawn into God's family and rescued from the effects of sin lies ahead. The harvest is still to come. Now is the time for waiting.

But to help us cope with the frustration of this waiting period, we're given the firstfruits of the harvest right here and now.

It's one thing for the farmer's little daughter to look at an empty barn in the summertime wondering if there's ever going to be anything in it. Week after week, she looks in and finds it still empty. She wonders whether the drought has destroyed the crops, or disease has wiped it all out, or maybe even whether her father forgot to sow any seeds this year.

But imagine how her spirits are lifted when she looks in one day and sees a little pile of grain in the corner. It's not much in itself, but it makes all the difference. She knows now it is just a matter of time before that barn is full to overflowing!

That is what the Spirit is to us. His presence in our lives is our God-given assurance that it's just a matter of time before the overflowing harvest of God's blessings fills our experience.

> ➤ The Spirit is a 'deposit' guaranteeing God's riches will follow.

Anyone who's booked a holiday (or a camp or a conference) or rented a property (or bought one) is probably familiar with the idea of the 'non-returnable deposit'. It's not the whole amount that's payable, but it functions to make it highly unlikely that you'll back out!

Handing over a deposit is a way of saying: 'I'm serious about this. You can bank on me following through with the balance'.

That's what God is saying to us when he gives us his Spirit.

> …God has given us the Spirit as a deposit, guaranteeing what is to come (2 Corinthians 5:5).

That again is what the Spirit is to us. When we begin to experience his work in our lives, we know we can bank on the full riches God is planning to give us.

It all adds up to one thing. The Spirit gives clear eyes to our hearts. Under his influence, we will open our eyes, raise our gaze and dismiss distraction. We will find a new horizon. As we are gripped by God's Spirit, our values will become the values of heaven. Our priorities will become those of the new creation.

Money, career, reputation, comfort and all the other idols of this world will become less sweet in their attraction. Their lure will be less powerful. Because our sights will be set more and more firmly on the wonder of what is to come.

We will live with a focus on the future and with hearts of hope.

FULL HEARTS

Learning to drive involves responding quickly and appropriately to what lies ahead. Will you brake, change lane, indicate or accelerate? Any half-decent instructor will tell you: how you act depends on what you see in front of you.

Learning to *live* is much the same. The same Spirit who trains your heart's *eyes* to look ahead, also trains your heart's *decisions* and even your heart's *instincts* to respond to what lies in the road out in front.

And make no mistake. We need the help!

Living a life that pleases God is hard, right? Wrong. It's not hard. It's impossible. It cannot be done.

Not without the Spirit, anyway.

> Those who are in the realm of the flesh cannot please
> God (Romans 8:8).

But when someone follows Jesus, everything changes. So
here's the very next sentence Paul writes:

> You, however, are not in the realm of the flesh, but are in
> the realm of the Spirit (Romans 8:9).

The Spirit makes all the difference. Without him, the
decisions and instincts of our hearts – and therefore the
way we speak and act – will be primarily self-serving
and God-ignoring, or even God-defying. But with the
fulfilment of what was promised back in Ezekiel 36:26 –
new hearts that come with the new Spirit – living God's
way is finally possible.

He's not called the 'Holy' Spirit for nothing.

A changed heart, brought about by the Spirit, will
show itself in a changed life. A holy life.

That changed *includes* the area of our lives that many
associate particularly with the Spirit: the area of our emotions. The Spirit can lead us to hate our sin. To be ashamed
of our track records. To be frustrated with ourselves.

Or more positively the Spirit may work in us to marvel
at Jesus. To be overwhelmed by his love. To be enraptured
by his grace and his goodness.

He might lead us to a genuine excitement about being involved in God's plans. To be just thrilled when we
hear news of his kingdom growing. And overjoyed when
we see someone we know displaying signs of deepening
discipleship.

The Spirit can change our emotions around alright.

But he doesn't stop at the emotions. He's interested in producing change in the whole of our lives. He wants to change my *character*.

That much is clear from one of the key ways the Bible describes what it looks like to 'live by the Spirit'.

> The acts of the flesh are obvious… But the fruit of the Spirit is love, joy, peace, forbearance, kindness, goodness, faithfulness, gentleness and self-control. Against such things there is no law (Galatians 5:19-23).

The choice of that particular phrase ('fruit of the Spirit') is interesting. It makes two things clear to us.

First, it tells us that these character qualities – love, joy, peace etc. – are the product of the Spirit's work in a person's heart.

The apple tree in my garden varies in its crop each year. But however much I take it for granted – and sadly I do! – what it produces is not random. It's a function of a number of factors: the nutrients in the soil, the rain and the sun, the competing vegetation around and the pruning regime. Most of all, it's a function of the original type of tree that was planted in the first place.

It's not random. Fruit doesn't just appear out of nowhere. And it's the same with character qualities in the believer's life. You don't just spontaneously become a better, more attractive, more Christ-like person. Life-change is evidence of the Spirit at work from the inside out.

'FRUITS OF THE SPIRIT'?

Christians sometimes talk about 'the fruits of the Spirit', referring to the passage in Galatians 5. It's clearly not accurate: the phrase used is 'the fruit of the Spirit'. But does one little 's' really matter? Are we getting a little fussy here?

There are two main problems with talking about 'the fruits of the Spirit'.

1. It implies that these nine qualities are a definitive list of what the Spirit is out to produce in a believer's life. But there are in fact a number of other lists of desirable character qualities given in the New Testament (e.g. 1 Corinthians 13:4-8 and Colossians 3:12-16) as well as numerous further indications of what our lives should look like. The phrase 'fruit of the Spirit' may not be used in those places, but there's no doubt that all these certainly are fruit of the Spirit: they're displays of the Spirit's work in the life of God's children as he makes us more like Jesus.

2. It focusses attention on the character quality itself, rather than where it comes from. In English, the word 'fruit' is not just the singular version of 'fruits' (one orange rather than ten oranges). It also speaks of a connection to the source or cause (my pay cheque is the fruit of a hard day's work). In fact it is the whole Christian life – marked by these nine qualities and a number of others besides – that is the fruit of the Spirit. That is the point of the expression. Christian character flows from the Spirit's work.

It seems like a small and insignificant shift – from 'fruit' to 'fruits' – but it can really change our way of thinking if we're not careful!

Second, as well as drawing attention to the source of Jesus-like character, the phrase 'fruit of the Spirit' tells us that these character qualities are good for other people.

Right through the Bible, fruit-bearing trees are a sign of God's blessing. Why is that? It's not just that they're a pretty sight to enjoy. It's that they nourish and sustain human life.

A Spirit-renewed heart will show itself in bringing benefit to others.

That's clear as soon as you start to ponder the fruit. How can I truly love without someone else profiting? What is kindness without bringing assistance to another in some way? When did gentleness ever fail to have some beneficial impact?

But there's more. When I display the fruit of the Spirit, not only do I benefit the person I'm facing (because I'm patient with them or self-controlled in what I say etc.), I also benefit the watching world. I'm advertising Jesus to them. And when a whole community is displaying this fruit, that advertisement is a powerful one.

CAN'T LOSE

How confident can a believer be that their future lies with Jesus in glory?

It's not uncommon for Christians to approach that question in a similar way to whether they'll get through their exams, or get the kind of job they want, or get married: there's a decent chance it'll all work out, but a number of factors could put a spanner in the works.

Maybe I'll give up on my faith. Maybe I'll mess up so badly I'll forfeit my chance to be forgiven. Maybe even now I feel God has given up on me. Maybe my constant struggle with temptation makes me feel I'm not a true Christian.

Maybe…

It's easy to feel that your spiritual future still lies in the balance.

And that's even before you get to some of those warnings in Hebrews. Or Jesus' parable of the sower and the seed.

The Bible encourages us to look outside ourselves – not inside – to work out whether we will indeed participate in glory. We're to look at the work of Jesus and the faithful commitment of God and indeed his verdict on our spiritual status more than at our own performance.

> My sheep listen to my voice; I know them, and they follow me. I give them eternal life, and they shall never perish; no one will snatch them out of my hand (John 10:27-28).

> In all my prayers for all of you, I always pray with joy… being confident of this, that he who began a good work in you will carry it on to completion until the day of Christ (Philippians 1:4, 6).

> For I am convinced that neither angels nor demons, neither the present nor the future, nor any powers, neither height nor depth, nor anything else in all creation, will be able to separate us from the love of God that is in Christ Jesus our Lord (Romans 8:38-39).

For all the warnings and urgings we find in the Bible, one thing's pretty clear: everyone who is genuinely born again and who has been brought into the family of God will make it to the finish line. It's a done deal. 100 per cent secure. The Father will not let them go.

If you've really started, you will certainly finish.

Ah, but there's the question. It's still hanging there, waiting for an answer.

'Have I in fact really started?'

Cue the final great work of the Spirit. Among all the other things he does in us and for us, he stills our flapping hearts and calms our anxious nerves on this question.

In Romans 8 – a chapter that's already been very helpful to us in a number of areas – we hear of this role.

> The Spirit himself testifies with our Spirit that we are God's children. Now if we are children, then we are heirs – heirs of God and co-heirs with Christ (Romans 8:16-17).

Adoptions were not uncommon in Ancient Rome. But they needed to be verifiable. The stakes were high: an adopted child could claim to be heir to a valuable estate. So there was no room for doubt. Rome's solution was a law that every adoption had to be witnessed by seven individuals, each of whom could then testify to the person's claim to be child and heir.

But what about for children of God?

If you want to know whether you've really got a place at the Father's table, then Paul's encouragement here is to look for evidence of the Spirit's work in your life. Then you will have your answer.

- Do you pray to God your Father?

- Do you care about pleasing Jesus or are you grateful to him for what he's done?

- Do you find you open the Bible – and benefit from it?

- Do you want other people to know about how they can be rescued from their sin?

- Do you find that you approach decisions – and maybe life itself – differently from people around you (or from the person you once were)?

- Do you struggle with temptation (as opposed to just giving in to it straight away without a thought)?

- Do you care about other Christians?

- Do you long for the life to come?

If you can answer some of those questions with at least a tentative yes, then it sounds like the Spirit has begun his work in you and has brought you to the family table of God.

That's the Spirit testifying that that you are God's child and heir. And remember: what God has started, he will finish. You can be sure of that!

It means that our confidence in this glorious inheritance is not misplaced. Our hearts can look to the future with security and assurance.

Or – to put it another way – you can't lose!

RESPONDING

An inert human body lying on an African plain will soon see the vultures beginning to gather. But when that man stands up and starts walking, those vultures will be on their way. The poise and direction of the man setting out on his journey convince the vultures that there is real life here. And so they scatter and look elsewhere for their next meal.

Hope – that precious work of the Spirit – is the spiritual lifeblood of the Christian believer.

Without it, we become easy prey for various forms of spiritual attack. But with it, we have what we need to stand up to them and send them on their way.

So three suggestions for keeping in step with the Spirit's work in our hearts:

1. Allow your heart of hope to ward off distraction.

The world around us has any number of attractions competing for our hearts. Money, reputation, material comfort, success and family all woo us and promise us ultimate fulfilment and satisfaction. But if we deliberately keep the eyes of our hearts trained on our glorious inheritance, we will find these things lose their allure by comparison. And we'll be saved from the danger of putting God second to something or someone far less worthy.

So find ways – any ways you can – to cultivate a future focus. Meditate on heaven (take a sustained time turning over in your mind verses in the Bible which speak of what is to come). Use prompts in the day ('every time I see a cloud I'll think of the day when Jesus returns in the clouds'). Pray for God's help ('Lord keep me thinking about the future even when just getting through each day seems like enough for me!').

2. Allow your heart of godliness to fight disobedience.

There is nothing like knowledge and determination to help in the battle against sin. So get clear on the shape of the Christian life. And invite God to do his work changing you and moulding you by his Spirit.

Just a tip here: as you seek to foster godly character traits, you'll likely need the help of your spiritual community around you. The Spirit has a track record of using our brothers and sisters in Christ to produce his fruit in our lives.

So open your life up to the scrutiny of others. Make sure those around you know you're serious about becoming more like Jesus and that you want their input in stamping out ungodliness and nurturing the fruit of the Spirit.

3. Allow your heart of assurance to beat back doubt.

Satan is real and he is dangerous. *'Your enemy the devil prowls around like a roaring lion, looking for someone to devour'* (1 Peter 5:8). He's out to rob Christians of their spiritual confidence and security. He can spot his prey a mile off: those who are wavering or unsure about their spiritual status. They are easy pickings for him; he's already chalking up another victory before he even gets to work.

So if you're a spiritual navel-gazer (constantly examining your feelings and performance and judging your spiritual security according to what you see there), then stop it! Learn to look outside yourself – to the completed work of Christ, the unfailing faithfulness of the Father and the reassurances given in the Bible by the Spirit. Satan is no match for the Christian believer who is looking in the right direction.

CONCLUSION

EVERY time you step outside your front door and walk along the road, there are two types of movement your body can engage in. One is the amble. There's no particular rush. No particular place you need to be anytime soon. You can stop and start at will. Listen to the birds, admire a cloud formation, pause for a chat with your neighbour. It's a free and unconstrained walking.

The second type is probably more common, though. It's walking to a pace – one that is set for you. It could be a physical pace-setter: you're walking with someone beside you, or in the middle of a big crowd, so you need to move together. Or it could be a pace-setter you can't see: a schedule that demands you be at work by a particular time, a concern not to arrive too early for your date, or even just the beat of the music in your ears.

In what is probably the very earliest book of the New Testament, the apostle Paul urged his Christian readers to live their whole lives as those who walk to a pace.

Since we live by the Spirit, let us keep in step with the Spirit (Galatians 5:25).

Now that you've spent a while discovering, or perhaps rediscovering, what the Spirit is about, can I urge you to follow Paul's instruction? As a dancer keeps in step with her partner, or a soldier keeps in step with his column, or a runner keeps in step with her coach, aim to live your life as one who keeps in step with the Spirit.

Allow him to set the pace for you.

Follow his lead.

Keep in step with the Spirit's purposes. Discern what he's seeking to do in your life – and the lives of others – and work with him, not against him.

Keep in step with the Spirit's priorities. Discern where his own focus lies – especially in bringing glory to Jesus – and direct your own gaze in the same direction.

And keep in step with the Spirit's person. Discern his value as a member of the Godhead – a 'he' rather than an 'it' – and give thanks to the Father often for the gift that he is to you.

As you go about your life, make your decisions, think through your priorities, react to your circumstances and ponder the realities of life, keep in step with the Spirit!

Big God

How to approach SUFFERING, spread the GOSPEL, make
DECISIONS and PRAY in the light of a God who really is in
the DRIVING SEAT of the world

Orlando Saer

ISBN 978-1-78191-294-2

Christian Focus Publications

Our mission statement –

STAYING FAITHFUL

In dependence upon God we seek to impact the world through literature faithful to His infallible Word, the Bible. Our aim is to ensure that the Lord Jesus Christ is presented as the only hope to obtain forgiveness of sin, live a useful life and look forward to heaven with Him.

Our books are published in four imprints:

CHRISTIAN
FOCUS

Popular works including biographies, commentaries, basic doctrine and Christian living.

CHRISTIAN
HERITAGE

Books representing some of the best material from the rich heritage of the church.

MENTOR

Books written at a level suitable for Bible College and seminary students, pastors, and other serious readers. The imprint includes commentaries, doctrinal studies, examination of current issues and church history.

CF4•K

Children's books for quality Bible teaching and for all age groups: Sunday school curriculum, puzzle and activity books; personal and family devotional titles, biographies and inspirational stories – because you are never too young to know Jesus!

Christian Focus Publications Ltd,
Geanies House, Fearn, Ross-shire,
IV20 1TW, Scotland, United Kingdom.
www.christianfocus.com